Hawaii Cooks

Hawaii Cooks

FLAVORS FROM Roy's PACIFIC RIM KITCHEN

Roy Yamaguchi

WITH Joan Namkoong

Food Photography by Maren Caruso

TEN SPEED PRESS

Berkeley / Toronto

Ten Speed Press
PO Box 7123
Berkeley, California 94707
www.tenspeed.com

Distributed in Australia by Simon and Schuster Australia, in Canada by Ten Speed Press Canada,
in New Zealand by Southern Publishers Group, in South Africa by Real Books, in Southeast Asia
by Berkeley Books, and in the United Kingdom and Europe by Airlift Book Company.

Jacket and text design by Elizabeth Stromberg
Food and prop styling by Erin Quon and Kim Konecny
Plate on page 95 provided by Tommy Bahama

Library of Congress Cataloging-in-Publication Data

Yamaguchi, Roy, 1956–
  Hawaii cooks : flavors from Roy's Pacific Rim kitchen / Roy Yamaguchi,
with Joan Namkoong.
      p. cm.
Includes index.
  ISBN 1-58008-454-0 (hardcover)
  1. Cookery, Hawaiian. I. Namkoong, Joan. II. Roy's East-West kitchen (Television program).
III. Title.

  TX724.5.H3 Y26   2003
  641.59969–dc21
                                        2002015182

First printing, 2003
Printed in China

1 2 3 4 5 6 7 8 9 10 – 07 06 05 04 03

Contents

**FOREWORD: THE SHOW
AND THE BOOK** / viii

INTRODUCTION: DEFINING MY STYLE / 1

PANTRY / 11

Flavors
Salty / 12
Sweet / 18
Sour, Tart, and Acidic / 22
Bitter / 24
Hot and Spicy / 25
Oceany / 29
Herbs and Spices / 31

Core Ingredients
Fish and Seafood / 36
Vegetables / 40
Tofu / 46
Starches / 47
Meats / 51
Ingredients to Add Richness / 52

RECIPES / 57

Appetizers, Small Plates, and Cocktails
Wok-Charred Edamame / 62
Aku Tataki / 63
Shrimp on a Sugar Cane Stick with
Pineapple-Mango Jam / 64
Spicy Chicken Wings / 66
Shrimp and Scallop Spring Rolls with
Champagne-Caviar Sauce / 67
Seafood Full Moon Dumplings with Crispy Ogo / 68
Molded Sushi with Unagi and Spicy Crab / 70
Crab and Taro Cakes with Béarnaise Sauce / 72
Chuck's Lamb Chops Pupu / 73
Pineapple Vodka / 74
Bloody Mary / 74

Salads
Roasted Duck Salad with Deep-Fried Tofu
and Mango / 78
Warm Tofu Salad of Wilted Greens
and Macadamia Nuts / 80
Ahi Salad with Miso Dressing / 82
Cured Salmon and Tomato Salad / 83
Seared Scallop Salad with Mangoes and
Fruit Vinaigrette / 84
Pickled Mango Vinaigrette / 86

Entrées

Grilled Chuck Steak with Pad Thai–Style Noodles / 90

Asian-Style Spicy Peppercorn Steak / 92

Portuguese-Style Steak Sandwich with
  Spicy Soy Dipping Sauce / 93

Lamb Steaks with Okinawan Sweet Potato Mash
  and Apple-Curry Sauce / 94

Mediterranean-Style Lamb with Crispy Ginger / 96

Roast Pork with Caramelized Pineapple / 97

Kalua Pork with Taro Sauce and
  Tofu-Yuba Stir-Fry / 98

Char Siu Pork Chops with Black Bean Sauce
  and Stir-Fried Vegetables / 100

Tuscan-Style Pasta with White Beans and Pork / 102

Salt-Crusted Cornish Game Hen with
  Thai Black Rice Risotto / 103

Steamed Chicken Breast with Vegetables and
  Soy Vinaigrette / 105

Pan-Seared Chicken with Honey Sauce,
  Couscous, and Vegetables / 106

Hawaiian Plate Lunch: Macaroni Salad, Shichimi
  Chicken, Thai Pineapple Rice, and
  Barbecue Salmon / 109

MediterAsian Saffron Chicken / 111

Thai-Style Deep-Fried Mullet with Coconut-Curry Sauce
  and Pineapple Fried Rice / 112

Ponape Pepper–Crusted Shutome on
  Cassoulet of Offal / 114

Mahimahi with Citrus Sauce, Apple Bananas, and
  Macadamia Nuts / 116

Lemon Grass–Crusted Hawaiian Shutome and
  Thai Peanut Sauce / 117

Chinese-Style Whole Steamed Fish / 118

Steamed Opakapaka and Salmon with
  Shrimp Mousse / 120

Golden Shrimp-Stuffed Tofu / 121

Fresh Pasta with Shrimp, Pancetta,
  Anchovy, and Garlic / 122

Vietnamese-Style Cold Udon with Shrimp / 124

Shrimp and Clam Linguine with Chile, Lemon Grass,
  and Black Bean Sauce / 126

Tea-Infused Shrimp Sauté / 127

Shrimp Risotto / 128

Crab with Vanilla Sauce / 129

Hawaiian Cioppino and Crostini with
  Eastern Rouille / 131

Kona Cold Lobster with Spicy Mango Sauce / 133

Stir-Fried Lobster with Spicy Garlic and
  Black Pepper Sauce / 134

Desserts

Lilikoi Pudding Cake / 138

Hawaiian Creamsicle Panna Cotta and Brown
   Sugar–Caramel Sauce / 140

Macadamia Nut Tart with Sugar Crust / 141

Chocolate Mousse / 142

Coconut Panna Cotta / 143

Minted Mango Martini Float with
   Crystallized Ginger / 144

White Pirie Mango Tart / 146

Hot Chocolate Soufflé / 147

Basics

Chicken Stock / 150

Toasted Coconut Flakes / 150

Sautéed Garlic and Garlic Oil / 151

Sautéed Ginger and Ginger Oil / 151

Mangoes / 151

Mung Bean Noodles / 152

Caramelized Pineapple / 152

Toasted Rice Powder / 153

Toasted Sesame Seeds / 153

Sautéed Shallots and Shallot Oil / 153

Shrimp Stock / 154

Teriyaki Sauce / 154

Tomatoes / 155

Basic Tomato Sauce / 155

Taro Leaves / 156

Veal Stock and Demi-Glace / 156

ACKNOWLEDGMENTS / 157

ABOUT THE AUTHOR / 158

INDEX / 160

Foreword: The Show and the Book

It has been just over a decade since *Hawaii Cooks with Roy Yamaguchi* first aired on public television. The theme of that episode was "East Meets West in Hawaii" and it featured a fashion designer, an architect, and local painter Mark Kadota—three artists who exemplify Roy's east-west style of cooking in their own work. We also included a story on an aquaculture shrimp farm on Oahu's north shore. Ten years ago, this idea of bringing together food and art, intermingled with stories on Hawaii's history and culture, challenged the notion of what a cooking show should be. At the time, cooking shows were mostly studio productions featuring lots of demonstration and instruction. But Roy and I wouldn't have it any other way.

Anyone who's ever spent time in Hawaii knows that food is a pervasive and essential part of life here. Our diverse heritage of Asian and Pacific cultures, where food is often the center of celebrations, religious ceremonies, and traditions, as well as the focal point of family gatherings, makes eating and the preparation of food an integral part of daily life.

Although he was born in Japan, Hawaii is a significant part of Roy's life. This is home; his father is from here and Roy's paternal grandfather owned a general store in Wailuku, Maui. Many childhood summers were spent in Honolulu and Maui visiting relatives, and of course eating lots of local food. Our food, like Hawaii itself, is a mixture of Western and Asian influences infused with native Hawaiian ingredients and sensibilities. This is why Roy's signature style of cooking combining Asian, European, and Pacific flavors comes so naturally to him.

His palate and his cooking are greatly influenced by the memories of foods he ate as a child in Hawaii and Japan, his culinary education, and his early professional career working with chefs Jean Berteranou and Michel Blanchet. When Roy calls his food "Hawaiian fusion cuisine," he means much more than a blending of flavors; fusion to Roy combines the tastes and recollections of the great meals prepared by his father and grandfather. His flavor combinations and unique style of cooking are natural extensions of Roy and the foods he likes to eat.

And I guess that's why it all tastes so good, because Roy's cooking comes from his heart and honestly speaks to who he is. I think all great chefs have a generosity of spirit and a love of sharing that is expressed in the most basic of human gestures—providing sustenance and nourishment for others. By sharing food, we share ourselves, and through that Roy hopes to impart a true sense of the diversity and richness that is Hawaii. To understand that is to understand Roy Yamaguchi's style of cooking.

It is in this spirit of sharing that this book was developed. Our intention is to provide insight on Roy's creative process and his philosophy of cooking by sharing his pantry, favorite ingredients, and flavors with you.

The best cuisine is created when you put a part of yourself into it, and I hope this glimpse into Roy's flavors and foods inspires you to share a bit of yourself in your next culinary endeavor. Enjoy!

—Melanie Kosaka, Executive Producer,
Hawaii Cooks with Roy Yamaguchi

Introduction: Defining My Style

My cooking reflects my Hawaiian roots. I grew up in Japan, but as a boy I spent summers on the island of Maui, where my grandfather ran a grocery store and family-style restaurant serving popular local foods. His cooking and that of my father, born and raised on Maui and the primary cook in our family, shaped my palate for the flavors and textures that I still seek. Those food memories include tomatoey Hawaiian-style beef stew with meltingly soft potatoes, served with a mound of white rice; starchy, earthy poi accompanied by lively salty salmon mixed with tomatoes and onions; chunky, fatty, garlicky, spicy Portuguese sausage with rice and eggs; crispy noodles topped with crunchy stir-fried vegetables accented with savory, smoky oyster sauce; and sashimi (raw sliced tuna) dipped in soy sauce and nose-tingling wasabi, relished for its gutsy flavor and meatlike texture. Whether it's savory, spicy, oily, rich, crunchy, or soft, this is the kind of food I want to eat.

For me eating and cooking are essentially the same: I like to cook what I eat and I like to eat what I cook. Mood is a factor in what I put together but underlying it all is a Hawaii state of mind, a bond with those childhood food experiences that has evolved into a Hawaiian fusion cuisine. My cooking encompasses my Asian background and my Western training as a chef, embracing a wide range of ingredients and cooking techniques from Europe, America, Asia, and beyond. It is a bold and flavorful style that takes advantage of the freshest and best products available in Hawaii and elsewhere.

Within this eclectic style, every dish I prepare incorporates three essential elements: flavor, texture, and visual appeal. Each component of a dish—protein, vegetable, starch, sauce, and garnish—contributes at least one of these elements to the overall outcome of a dish.

1

I don't play with food. I keep the main ingredient—a piece of beef, lamb, chicken, pork, fish—as true as possible, judiciously seasoned to enhance its flavor. Sauces act as the powerful flavor factor. Their intensity is derived from Asian ingredients like soy, garlic, ginger, and chile peppers, tempered with sweetness and sometimes mellowed with cream or butter. I always look for boldness in the balance, because I want the first bite you take to be as exciting as the last bite. I'm looking for the "wow" factor. At Roy's, I make sure eating is never boring.

The Basic Tastes

Salty, sweet, sour, and bitter are the four basic tastes we recognize with every bite of food. Mine is a salty palate; I don't crave sweet things. This doesn't mean that you'll find my food too salty, but it does indicate that my food will be savory with perhaps a hint of sweetness to round out the sharp edge of saltiness.

With salt, the taste buds are aroused and food takes on vitality; without it a piece of meat would be bland, a vegetable lifeless. Salt can even bring out sweetness in a piece of fruit. From the pantry list that follows, you will see a number of ways I add salt to food that often contribute another flavor dimension like smoky, briny, fishy, and even spicy.

Sweetness is perhaps the first taste to hit the taste receptors of the tongue and, used carefully, it will balance the saltiness inherent in many of the Asian sauces I use. Sweetness is also needed to temper acidity, tartness, and the heat of chiles.

Beyond flavor, sugar plays a role in the textural and visual qualities of food. A marinade that is thick and dense with sugar will stick to the surface of meats. When that meat is grilled, the sugar caramelizes and even burns, developing a nice charred surface that can have crispness as well as eye-appealing color.

Sour is hardly a taste to embrace on its own, but it is a vital part of the overall flavor sensation I seek. Sourness causes the taste receptors to pucker up so there always has to be an element that puts it in balance. The tartness and acidity of lemon, for example, balanced with the sweetness of sugar and the saltiness of soy sauce achieves a pleasant tanginess on the taste buds. This taste is perceived as refreshing and light.

A bitter component seems to set up the taste buds for the next flavor. It's almost as if bitterness cleanses the palate. That's why I find a Campari and soda or Angostura bitters and soda very refreshing before starting a meal. Likewise, bitter greens in a salad can enhance the tasty properties of other ingredients on the plate, allowing them to be brisk and vibrant.

Umami, the Fifth Taste

A Japanese term, *umami* is referred to as the fifth taste, alongside salty, sweet, sour, and bitter. It is not a specific flavor but an overall taste sensation that is characterized as savory, flavorful, and satisfying. *Umami* can involve mouth-feel and the sense of smell; together with taste it is a feeling of satiation in the mouth that is considered pleasant and delicious.

The taste sensation of *umami* is linked to amino acids and molecules that enhance the flavor of food and occur naturally in a wide variety of foods that we eat every day. It is the savoriness that results when you add manufactured monosodium glutamate, or MSG, to foods, a product used extensively in food production and as a seasoning.

When I think back to my childhood, MSG was always on the table, sprinkled on foods to add its characteristic earthy, savoriness to dishes. Fresh asparagus, soy sauce, and mayonnaise sprinkled with MSG is one of the classic combinations I grew up on; my palate is accustomed to searching for that savory element.

While I don't use manufactured MSG in any of my cooking, this difficult to define flavor element is naturally present in a number of ingredients like *konbu,* soy sauce, miso, shiitake mushrooms, Parmesan cheese, ripe tomatoes, *yuzu,* clam juice, demi-glace, and a host of foods we eat every day. But no single ingredient can produce the depth and savoriness I seek to create in my dishes; rather it is the selection and variety of ingredients that result in food that one might say encompasses *umami.*

Spicy Sensations

Spicy heat is not really a flavor but a sensation in the mouth that is part of the liveliness of many foods. I like to use a variety of fresh chiles and chile-based sauces and condiments, many of which add other flavor components as well as mouth-tingling heat.

When adding spicy heat, it is important to temper it a little so that the mouth is receptive to more than an initial burst of heat. Sugar will entice the mouth with its initial flavor impact: sweetness hits the tongue first in a palatable way then heat kicks in. Butter, cream, and coconut milk will coat the mouth with richness and lessen the impact of chiles on the nerve endings of the tongue. Eggs can also tame fiery chiles as part of a marinade or as a coating on foods, shielding the taste receptors from a potent assault.

Texture

When you take a bite of food, the first thing that comes into play is whether it is soft, crisp, light, chewy, or silky. Then you taste the flavors.

The mouth-feel of food is about how you taste food: soft foods linger on the tongue and their taste is diffused; crunchy foods are chewed on but don't remain long in the mouth; silky sauces permeate and coat the mouth with flavor. What makes a dish interesting and fun is to mix crispy with soft, crunchy with chewy, heartiness with lightness; the variation of texture within a dish is what creates interest and excitement from first bite to last.

The natural textures of different foods lend their qualities to my cooking. For crunch, there are a multitude of vegetables I cook on the crisp side like bok choy, bell peppers, carrots, snap peas, Chinese peas, green beans, cabbage, and broccolini. Raw salad greens like won bok (Chinese or napa cabbage), hearts of romaine, celery, cucumber, fennel, and sweet onions are frequently used. Nuts are naturally crunchy too.

I love the soft chewiness of Italian parsley dressed with a little olive oil and lemon juice; likewise the toothsome bite of greens like chicory, cilantro, and corn sprouts. Mushrooms have their own rubbery quality, as does tofu when it is deep-fried, both of which can replicate the hearty bite of beef for a vegetarian presentation.

For softness, I turn to baby greens and micro-greens, uncooked herbs like basil and *shiso,* and fruits like ripe papaya, mango, bananas, and avocado. I like the softness of well-cooked asparagus because it has more flavor than crunchy asparagus. There is the softness of starches like poi, mashed potatoes, sticky rice, and creamy polenta.

Slipperiness occasionally factors into my cooking, a moist quality that not everyone likes. But it has its place in coating the mouth to temper assertive flavors, like okra does in a spicy jambalaya. One of the most unique things to use in a salad is *yama imo* (mountain yam). Grind it up and it is pasty; when it is cut into julienne strips, it is crunchy but slippery.

Different cooking methods create textures too. Searing a piece of meat, chicken, or fish promotes caramelization on the surface, creating a crisp, chewy texture as well as golden brown color. I like to deep-fry soft foods like potato, taro, spinach, artichokes, basil, and *shiso* for a hard, crusty bite. *Panko,* Japanese bread crumbs, deep-fried to a golden brown, provides a crunchy coating for tender vegetables or delicate fish.

Starches can be soft or hard, depending on how you prepare them. Mashed potatoes, for example, can be whipped by hand to be light and creamy but put them in a food processor with lots of cream and butter and you get a thick, starchy, rich-tasting dish. Fry potatoes or cooked noodles and they take on a crispy exterior and soft interior. For garnishes, I like to purée day-old rice with water and bake it into brittle thin sheets; soft tortillas, baked or fried, and bread made into crostini are useful in adding a textural variation.

When it comes to creating silkiness and creaminess in the mouth, butter, cream, or coconut milk will coat the tongue, spreading flavor sensations throughout the palate. The smooth, unctuous mouth-feel of these ingredients paired with the assertive, sometimes coarse seasonings of the Asian pantry form an intriguing and elegant sensation.

Every component in a dish I create contributes a tactile quality that plays upon your senses to extend the excitement of each bite of food. As flavor kicks in, the diner is engaged in more than just eating: it is a complete sensory experience.

Visual Appeal

Visual appeal in cooking comes naturally to me, ingrained perhaps by the Japanese aesthetic in which I grew up.

There always has to be color in my dishes to make them more attractive and appetizing. Let's face it, a piece of cooked meat is gray and dull unless you sear it well and caramelize it to a golden brown. But add some colorful vegetables, a drizzle of herb-flavored oil, perhaps some bright yellow corn sprouts, and the dish becomes a feast for the eyes.

It can be a challenge to weave in color because sometimes colorful products may not fit the dish. I like to use strips of red and yellow bell peppers, for example, but they don't always fit an elegant dish because they can appear to be chunky and large. Green and red lettuces can lend their colors but their softer texture must be in context too. Briny bright orange fish roe would easily be lost in a seafood- and tomato-based pasta sauce.

Some of the foods I use include red, yellow, green, and purple tomatoes; green and red lettuces; yellow corn sprouts; red and yellow bell peppers; red amaranth; purple and green micro-greens; and many of the interesting shapes and colors of herbs and vegetables. Okinawan sweet potato provides a deep purple tone; saffron and carrots lend a yellow-orange accent; and spinach bestows a bright green tint. Puréed beets or the cooking water from beets can color dressings and sauces. For a deep purple drizzle, reduce cabernet sauvignon and add a little sugar to mellow the resulting tartness and a dab of butter to make it silky.

Oil drizzles accentuate flavors and add color: curry oil for yellow, scallion oil for green, and beet oil for red. Black sesame seeds impart an Asian accent and a crunchiness not found in white sesame seeds. Garnishes of caviar and seaweed impart flavor, texture, and visual appeal all in one.

Besides color, there is the idea of dimension. While some may not like "towers" on a plate, I find that height adds visual interest. Main ingredients like steaks or fillets of fish are flat, so I layer the components. There may be a bed of mashed potatoes or greens beneath a piece of meat or fish, stacked with garnishes and surrounded by sauces and drizzles. The three-dimensional quality helps to fulfill your taste buds: the colors, textural components, the foods themselves, the drizzles and garnishes work together to communicate an excitement soon to be matched by the bold flavors of the first bite. There's energy and liveliness there.

How It All Comes Together

The creation of exciting food is about drawing on all my food experiences—all the dishes and foods I have tasted over time. As a chef, I have a visual bank of flavors, textures, and colors in my mind and with these impressions I can envision the taste and see the outcome of a dish. To visualize in this way means going through the steps of cooking, thinking about each ingredient, what happens to it as it cooks, and what I want the final outcome to be. Do I want something light or heavy, subtle or bold, delicate or robust? Then I work my way backward. Here's what I was thinking for the Roasted Duck Salad with Deep-Fried Tofu and Mango (page 78):

There were two considerations for the duck: the leg should be roasted, well-cooked, and tender while the breast needs to be crispy, chewy, medium rare, and moist. I seasoned the leg with salt and pepper, nothing like garlic and ginger because they would burn and become bitter. The leg starts in a skillet with the meat side down to brown well, then is turned so the skin side can sear and brown. I then transfer it to the oven to cook until well done.

The breast is a different matter. The fatty skin crisps beautifully as it is pan seared; I know that salty and crispy makes duck more palatable even if it's fatty. The breast meat cooks only briefly to keep it medium rare, crisp on the outside but soft and chewy on the inside.

The duck requires a strong and assertive dressing to cut through the fattiness. *Yuzu* and lemon juice provide a pungency and tart acidity to overcome the fat while adding a refreshing citrus note. Sugar balances the tartness as well as the saltiness of the soy sauce, while sesame oil adds its toasty flavor to mellow the salt of the soy sauce.

The greens must be crispy and flavorful enough to stand up to the duck and the strong dressing. Chicory has crunch and subtle bitterness in the stems. Mango pulls together many elements, adding sweetness to balance the assertive dressing, lightness opposite the heartiness and richness of the duck, creaminess against the crunchy chicory and crispy duck, and of course, its eye-appealing yellow-orange color.

Shiitake mushrooms are hearty like a steak with a nice chewiness, but because they are fresh they have a light earthy flavor that complements the robustness of the duck. The tofu is there for fun, not contributing much in flavor, but by deep-frying it I can add some chewy texture and golden brown color.

This dish is about strong and bold flavors and hearty and delicate textures laced with appetizing color. It's about assertive and fulfilling elements that will fill you mentally, therefore physically. It is not a rich dish in the sense of unctuous ingredients but the variations of tastes and textures will excite the taste buds and keep them interested until the last morsel is consumed.

Each of my dishes is created with one goal in mind—to satisfy the person eating it. Using my experience as a chef, my hands, and my sense of taste to make something good that people respond to immediately is what makes cooking so rewarding.

Pantry

I think of ingredients in two different categories: those that create flavor and those that carry flavor in a dish. Obviously, these latter, core ingredients provide flavor in their own right as well, but the flavor components serve that primary purpose. In this pantry section, the ingredients that create flavor are organized by their taste characteristic: salty, sweet, sour, bitter, spicy, oceany, and so on. Core ingredients are organized by type: fish, vegetables, starches, meats, and so on.

This section is not at all intended as an exhaustive list. What I include here are those flavor elements that form the basis of the tastes found in my cooking, along with a selection of core ingredients that I turn to again and again. I hope these serve as inspiration for you to experiment with your own favorite flavors and textures.

The majority of the ingredients in this list will be available in Asian grocery stories—start with a Chinese grocery, and go to Vietnamese, Laotian, or Thai markets from there. Sushi bars are a good source for Japanese products; even a neighborhood restaurant could supply you with an item or two.

Flavors

The flavor components in my pantry are a true reflection of my heritage and the memories I have of meals prepared by my parents and extended family of aunts and uncles. These flavors speak to who I am and what I like to eat, and are not meant as any type of ingredient guide or directory.

Salty, sweet, sour, bitter, and hot and spicy are the flavor components that make up the sense of taste. While we all might have different palates—what is very salty to one person may be mild to someone else—these categories break down taste to its basic elements. To these five basic flavors, I have added a sixth: oceany. This is my own category; it is not a standard flavor component but is an integral part of my cooking. Having grown up in Japan surrounded by the ocean and spending summer vacations in Hawaii, the unique salty-sweet flavors derived from the sea are so much a part of my cooking that I felt this sublime taste deserved a flavor category of its own.

Salty

Salt is the most basic of seasonings, essential to the overall taste of food and vital to the savoriness of my cooking. In adding saltiness to foods, don't always just reach for plain table salt. There are so many ways to add this taste to foods; miso, soy sauce, fish sauce, and anchovies are some of the products I use to add saltiness to my cooking.

ANCHOVIES

Use these tiny fish preserved in salt for pastas, sauces, and dressings to add saltiness and savory flavor at the same time. Because they are soft, anchovies disappear into cooked sauces leaving their essence to add depth without being too fishy. Sometimes anchovies can be too salty; soak them in cool water for 15 to 20 minutes, drain, pat dry, and use. I use both the salt-cured and oil-packed anchovies. If they come in tins, transfer them to a covered container for storage in the refrigerator.

FERMENTED BLACK BEANS

Soybeans that have been cooked, salted, and fermented become black, soft, salty, and aromatic. Add fermented black beans along with garlic and ginger to stir-fried, steamed, or braised dishes. (In dressings they can be too pungent and discolor the dish.) These beans can be used straight from their plastic bag or jar as a salty component in seafood, meat, and poultry dishes; they marry well with vegetables like asparagus and broccoli. Sometimes I soak the black beans in water for a few minutes before use to reduce the saltiness; mashing and chopping the beans will release more of their flavor. Fermented black beans can be stored in a covered container in the refrigerator indefinitely.

FISH SAUCE

Fish sauce is a little deceiving: a whiff and a taste make it seem like it would have a very fishy, salty flavor, but it really isn't as salty as it may seem. Once you have added other ingredients and mellowed the fish sauce with a little sugar, you might have to add a little salt. I like fish sauce because of its underlying fish flavor but its pungent aroma dissipates when you cook it.

The clear brown liquid is made by fermenting fish in brine for several months in the sun and then straining the liquid. Known as *nuoc mam* in Vietnam, *nam pla* in Thailand, and *patis* in the Philippines, it is as essential to cooking in Southeast Asia as soy sauce is in China, Korea, and Japan. Like soy sauces, there are many nuances in fish sauce depending on its origin and the care with which it is made. It can be stored in the pantry indefinitely.

HOISIN

Hoisin is a reddish brown sauce made of mashed soybeans, sugar, garlic, Chinese five-spice powder, a hint of chile, and red rice as a coloring agent. Its salty-sweet-spicy flavor is potent but it is ideal for barbecue marinades and roasted meats and poultry; I like to combine it with veal stock, ginger, garlic, sesame oil, and green onions. Thick like jam or runny like honey, hoisin adds thickness and flavor to dressings and is often used as a condiment diluted with a little sesame oil. Hoisin is sold in jars or cans; store in a covered jar in the refrigerator indefinitely.

MISO

Soybeans form the basis of this fermented paste that is an important seasoning ingredient in the foods of Japan and Korea. The type of grain mixed with the puréed soybeans and *koji* (yeast mold) distinguishes the color and flavor of miso. Flavors range from sweet to salty, mild to robust, and the texture can be smooth or chunky.

Red miso, made with rice and soybeans, is robust in flavor, tends to be very salty, and can be smooth or chunky. This type of miso is best used in marinades for meat, poultry, and hearty fish.

For marinades, dressings, and sauces I usually use *shiro* or white miso, actually yellowish, made with rice and soybeans. It is sweet and mild in flavor and tends to be smooth in texture. Miso pairs well with mirin (page 19) to diminish its saltiness; in some preparations, mixing miso with an egg will do the trick.

Moromiso is a strong, pungent, chunky miso often served as a dipping sauce with cucumbers; I sometimes use it in place of red or white miso.

OYSTER SAUCE

This dark brown, thick, full-flavored sauce is made of dried oysters, salt, and water. Its salty taste relates to its quality: generally more expensive brands tend to be less salty and more flavorful. There is a hint of smokiness in this briny-flavored sauce; the addition of caramel adds a little sweetness. Oyster sauce can be used straight from the bottle in marinades, sauces, and stir-fry dishes but always add a little sugar to take away the salty edge. Once opened, a bottle of oyster sauce should be stored in the refrigerator where it will last indefinitely.

RED THAI CURRY PASTE

When you think of a Thai curry paste, spiciness comes to mind. But this paste is salty and in fact you taste the salt before the spiciness when you put a little on your tongue. Red Thai curry paste gets its saltiness from the shrimp paste included in this savory mixture of red chiles, coriander root and seeds, garlic, shallots, kaffir lime leaves, lemon grass, and galangal.

Obviously I use it for more than just its saltiness; the herbal qualities and spiciness are just as important. Coconut milk is the natural partner: it helps temper the flavors and evens out the saltiness and heat of this ingredient.

SALT

Salt is the most basic of ingredients in cooking, enhancing the natural flavors of food and providing a textural component. When faced with the many varieties of salt I have to ask, "Am I using this salt primarily as a seasoning or for texture as well?"

The fine, free-flowing crystals of plain table salt are considered the saltiest and perhaps the most useful as a seasoning. Many chefs prefer kosher salt because it is a hard salt, "clean" in flavor, slightly coarser than table salt, and slightly less salty. Sea salts such as those from the coast of Brittany, France, or Maldon, England, tend to be coarser in texture, sometimes flaky, and range in color from white to gray. These sea salts are ideal as condiments, adding textural crunch to a dish and also their characteristic mineral flavor.

Alaea

Kosher   Coarse sea

In Hawaii, coarse sea salt granules are referred to as Hawaiian salt. It is a hard salt with a chewy, crunchy texture. *Alaea,* Hawaiian salt colored with red earth, often used too, is slightly less salty than the white Hawaiian salt. Salt gathering along the islands' shorelines has been a tradition for centuries, particularly at Hanapepe on the island of Kauai. It is here that the red earth is used to color the sea salt granules.

In my kitchen, regular table salt is used to season most dishes including stews, braised dishes, soups, even delicate fish. For heartier meats like steak, I use kosher or Hawaiian salt, which lend their textural qualities to the enhancement of flavor.

Table

SOY SAUCE

Soy sauce is one of five essential ingredients in my pantry (the others are salt, garlic, ginger, and sugar). There are many different kinds of soy sauce, some saltier than others, some more flavorful, some denser. After traveling in Asia, I often return home with a bag full of different soy sauces to experiment with in my cooking.

Soy sauce is the most popular and most widely used of Asian seasonings. It has been in use for over three thousand years to help preserve as well as season food. The Chinese invented this liquid made from naturally fermented soybeans, wheat, yeast, and salt, but it was the Japanese who refined it into a product that is aged and distilled through a natural brewing, process resulting in a mellow, aromatic, and savory sauce.

Soy sauces vary in color and saltiness. I generally use standard Japanese *shoyu* (soy sauce) because it tends to be mellower and more refined. Equal portions of soybeans and wheat make this soy sauce a little sweeter and less salty than Chinese light soy sauce, a thin but salty equivalent. In marinades, I prefer Kikkoman soy sauce, a little denser and saltier than the Yamasa soy sauce that I prefer with fish. The important thing to look for when buying a soy sauce is that it is naturally brewed, without caramel as an ingredient.

When I want an earthy, woody flavor in a stew or stir-fried dish, mushroom soy sauce fits the bill. In marinades, it lends a golden color to roasted meats and poultry. When I don't want color, especially in a dressing or sauce, *shiro shoyu* is used for its light color and sweeter flavor due to its higher proportion of wheat. Once a bottle has been opened the color begins to darken so it is best to use it quickly.

Soy sauce is assertive, so when I use it in marinades, for example, I temper the saltiness as much as possible with sugar but I try not to let sweetness take over. Another way to mellow the saltiness of soy sauce is to use eggs. For example, when eating the Japanese dish *sukiyaki,* hot morsels of soy-seasoned food are dipped in a raw egg before they are consumed. If you have a piece of soy-marinated food, you can soften the saltiness of the soy sauce by coating it in an egg batter for frying. An example of this is the Spicy Chicken Wings (page 66).

Soy sauce as a condiment or dipping sauce is essential to eating sashimi or raw fish. There are two theories to consider here: enjoy the natural taste of the fish (or any other food) with a light, thin soy sauce; or coat the morsel with a thick soy sauce that clings to the fish. Tamari, a soy sauce made without wheat, thick, dense, and full flavored, is sometimes my preference.

If soy sauce is just too salty on its own, try a reduced-sodium or lite soy sauce that still has the characteristic mellow flavor. It is more perishable so it should be stored in the refrigerator after opening.

In Japan, where I grew up, soy sauce is the base for sauces served with virtually everything. There are dozens of these sauces prepared commercially and available in markets. *Ponzu* is one, a mixture of soy sauce and tart citrus juice that can be used in marinades, dressings, and as a dipping sauce. Teriyaki is a sweet-salty soy-based marinade, sauce, and glaze used with meats, fish, and chicken. It is syrupy and dense due to the high proportion of sugar in the sauce. Teriyaki sauce is available in bottles but it is simple to make your own (page 154).

Kabayaki is another sweet-salty soy-based sauce, traditionally comprised of eel bones, soy sauce, mirin, and sugar, thickened and sweetened with a purée of apples. It is usually used to complement eel in sushi preparations (page 71).

THE ART OF SALTING

Salting a piece of food is about hand eye coordination and about visual taste and control. Grab some salt between your thumb and first two fingers and release little by little over a piece of food, moving your hand a few inches above the surface. The food itself will determine the amount of salt you need: its flavor, thickness, water content, and so on. Smaller-grained salt should be evenly distributed over the surface but you may not be able to do this with coarser-grained salt. For practice, salt a piece of food blindfolded; with practice salting will become natural, not forced.

Sweet

Sweet balances salt, acid, and the heat of chiles, and it contributes to the textural and visual qualities of food. I was raised on sweet-savory dishes—my mother prepared sukiyaki and teriyaki all the time when I was growing up. In my own cooking, I take advantage of the juxtaposition of salty and sweet over and over again.

FRUITS

Tropical fruits add an exotic flavor and sweetness that can temper spiciness and saltiness in a preparation while adding lightness to heavy and hearty combinations. I especially like to use low-acid golden pineapples and white Sugar Loaf pineapples, both very sweet with a hint of acidity. Seasonal lychee with its white juicy flesh adds a luscious grapelike note. Passion fruit is usually tart but when sweetened and made into syrup, it adds a distinctive tropical note to a dish.

Pineapples

The golden orange flesh of a mango lends its lively, peachy-citrusy-pineappley tropical flavor. In the hot, flat Waianae Valley along Oahu's leeward coast, the Suiso family nurtures their small but prolific Makaha Mango orchard. One day, I sat among the trees tasting their different varieties—Haden, Pirie, White Pirie, Mapulehu, Chinese, Pope, Garcia, Keitt, Momi K—each with their own distinctive flavor and texture. There's nothing better than eating a prime, ripe, juicy mango over the kitchen sink with juice running down your chin and arms. Truly, the best mangoes are in Hawaii in the summertime.

An apple banana can also add a tropical sweetness to dishes. This is a plump, short banana about half the size of a Bluefield banana. Grown in Hawaii, they are very popular and often preferred over other varieties because of their slightly tart but sweet flavor, and firm but creamy flesh.

Mangoes

Citrus fruits usually provide acidity except for the Kau orange, a juicy sweet variety grown on the southern tip of the island of Hawaii. It is a well-known fact that inside the mottled orangey green, ugly exterior, is the sweetest orange you can find.

HONEY

Honey's varied flavors and aromatic nuances are derived from the particular flower nectar that honeybees convert to thick sweet liquid. Age will also determine the strength of flavor: over time it becomes more robust and its color darkens from golden to brown. While honey's sweetness is desirable in sauces, marinades, and dressings, I have to consider its distinctive flavor too, and use it when appropriate. Always store honey at room temperature; if it should crystallize, warm the jar in a simmering pot of water.

MIRIN

In my cooking, sugar is often replaced with mirin, a syrupy, sweet liquid made from fermented glutinous rice and *shochu,* the Japanese distilled grain alcohol. *Hon* mirin (true mirin) is naturally brewed and has a 12 to 14 percent alcohol content. The alcohol is usually burned off in cooking, leaving the sweet flavor. *Aji* mirin is mirin with salt and corn syrup added and is not preferred.

Mirin's high sugar content tenderizes meats in marinades, produces a glaze on cooked foods, and adds its sweetness to sauces and dressings, especially those with soy sauce and miso. Store mirin in the refrigerator.

SAKE

Sake is Japanese rice wine, brewed from highly polished rice that is steamed, fermented with yeast, filtered, and aged. Its origins date back thousands of years to China but it became more refined in Japan. Hawaii once had its own sake breweries; today sake is made in Japan and some production is now happening in California and Oregon.

HAWAIIAN CHOCOLATE

In the mid-1980s, cacao trees were planted on the island of Hawaii where deep soil, abundant rainfall, and filtered sun provide optimum growing conditions. Colorful cacao pods are harvested throughout the year and the beans go through a lengthy process of fermentation, drying, roasting, grinding, and blending to produce the delicious chocolate we love to eat. Currently the Hawaiian Chocolate Factory in Kona, Hawaii, is the only producer of chocolate grown and processed in Hawaii.

As a cooking ingredient, sake can add its subtle flavor to marinades and sauces, just like a wine. I often use sake in place of white wine, especially when I want to add a hint of sweetness to a sauce.

As a beverage, sake is very compatible to my style of cooking. Ranging from sweet to dry with an alcohol content of 14 to 17 percent, sake can be thought of as a dry white wine with a lot less acidity. Served cold, sake is subtle and delicate and will complement fish, shellfish, pork, chicken, and a host of Asian seasonings.

SUGAR

White granulated cane sugar is an all-purpose sweetener and a staple of my pantry. It is almost always present in my cooking to take the edge off salty, sour, and spicy ingredients, balancing the sharpness but still allowing those tastes to predominate. A little sweetness allows the palate to be more receptive to these flavors and sensations.

Most often, I use plain sugar for sweetness because it has no other flavor component that can alter the taste of a dish. Sometimes honey, mirin, or palm sugar will be more appropriate, lending their specific flavor characteristics. I especially like the caramel undertones of palm sugar in combination with coconut milk and Thai curry pastes. This golden tan sugar is derived from the sap of coconut palm or sugar palm trees, collected like maple syrup then boiled down to a thick paste sold in jars. Palm sugar offers a mild caramel flavor in addition to its sweetness and it is used mostly in Southeast Asia to balance the saltiness of fish or soy sauce and the acidity of citrus juices. Palm sugar is sometimes called coconut sugar; in India it is known as jaggery.

Sugar cane

Brown

Turbinado

Granulated

Palm

In desserts, I sometimes use raw white sugar, a 100 percent Maui-grown and -processed sugar. Its granules are coarse and light tan in color; its flavor is sweet like granulated sugar but with a hint of molasses. Raw white sugar is lighter in color and flavor than turbinado sugar, another product of Maui. If you use a packet of sugar in the raw in your coffee, you are using raw white sugar from Hawaii.

A unique way to add sweetness to a savory dish is to use sugar cane sticks. Fresh sticks are difficult to find but canned ones are readily available in Asian grocery stores. They are very firm and fibrous (be sure to use a heavy, sharp knife to cut them) but you can chew on them for juicy sweetness. Leftover sticks can be placed in a plastic bag and frozen.

Sour, Tart, and Acidic

Sour, tart, and acidic elements play a role in the overall taste of a dish but must be balanced with sweet and salty flavors. Growing up in Japan, my dad used to take us to a Chinese restaurant once a month, and we would always order sweet-and-sour pork. I still love that sour-sweet combination. Tart or sour appetizers are a good way to start a meal since they stimulate the palate, just as having a glass of champagne is an excellent aperitif. Tart flavors can also serve as a palate cleanser. Whenever I eat sushi, I like to end with *ume*—sour pickled plum.

CITRUS

Citrus fruits like lemons, limes, and oranges contribute acidity and tartness as ingredients in marinades, sauces, and dressings, and as condiments. I always prefer to use freshly squeezed juices.

Yuzu, or Japanese citron, is usually prized more for its peel than its juice. The very sour juice has a hint of bitterness that I like to smooth with a little lemon or lime juice, sugar, and oil. Fresh *yuzu* is rarely available so I use bottled *yuzu* juice, which has a salty note to it that disappears when paired with soy sauce in a *ponzu* dip.

PICKLED GINGER JUICE

Gari is pickled ginger, served at sushi bars and often used as a garnish in my dishes. Once a container of *gari* is emptied, the remaining liquid can be used for sauces and dressings. The flavor of young ginger that has steeped in rice vinegar, salt, and sugar adds a unique tartness that can be mixed with oil for a dressing.

VINEGARS

There is a multitude of vinegars, each with a distinctive sour flavor derived from its source ingredient. The sourness or acetic acid can come from grapes to produce red or white wine, sherry, champagne, or balsamic vinegars. Apples produce cider vinegar; malted barley or oats result in malt vinegar.

A favorite of mine is rice vinegar, a clear, mild but acidic vinegar made from fermented rice and grains such as wheat, millet, and sorghum. It is sweeter than Western distilled and cider vinegars and less astringent on the tongue.

Sherry vinegar is derived from creamy, golden sweet sherry wines called olorosos that are fermented in casks to produce vinegar with raisiny qualities and depth of flavor. In the vinegar taste spectrum, sherry vinegar falls somewhere between balsamic and red wine vinegar.

Balsamic vinegar is made from Trebbiano grape juice, aged in successively smaller casks as its flavor becomes concentrated and fruity. True artisanal balsamic vinegar is aged for at least a dozen years. Commercially produced balsamic vinegar is usually a mixture of wine vinegar and caramel. This type of balsamic vinegar is best used in marinades, dressings, and as a cooking ingredient; the artisanal should be reserved for use as a condiment.

Raspberry, blueberry, and passion fruit vinegars are especially nice for dressings, adding their fruity essence along with their acidity. Such vinegars are also excellent when I want to deglaze a pan after cooking chicken or pork. A few tablespoons of fruit vinegar will loosen the bits that have accumulated in the pan; combined with demi-glace and butter, the acidity is diminished and the fruit essence shines.

Bitter

There are not many bitter foods I use since most people don't find it a pleasant flavor. Bitter can be quite effective in the overall taste scheme as long as the flavors are carefully balanced so no particular one is too overpowering. I like bitter and sweet, bitter and salty, and even bitter and spicy combinations. For me, bitter is a comforting taste sensation. As a kid, my mother would prepare bitter foods for me whenever I was sick. In Okinawa, where my mother is from, bitter melon is widely used and valued for its medicinal and healing properties.

BITTER MELON

This wrinkled, bumpy, green-skinned relative of the cucumber is very bitter but it is an interesting item in a stir-fry mixture. It requires a rich, spicy, and bold seasoning to mellow the bitterness as in Tofu-Yuba Stir-Fry (page 98).

GREENS

I am fond of certain greens like chicory, radicchio, and watercress in salads and I like to highlight them with hazelnut or walnut oil that also has a hint of bitterness.

I sometimes use raw mustard, kale, spinach, and chard greens in salads for a hint of bitterness. Cooked, these greens add flavor in fillings for dumplings and filled pastas.

Hot and Spicy

While there is little flavor in spicy heat, it is an exciting sensation for the mouth. Heat can drastically alter the taste of a dish, so it must always be carefully balanced. Too much, and the heat—not the flavor—dominates the food. In adding spiciness to food, you need to continually taste and taste!

CHILE OILS

Chile oils are vegetable oils infused with chile peppers over heat and strained. They can be quite potent, pack a lot of heat, and are used mostly as a condiment or last-minute seasoning, but rarely for cooking. I especially like *rayu,* sesame oil infused with chile peppers, sprinkled on at the end of cooking for flavor and heat. Chile oils are sold in glass bottles and should be stored in a cool area.

CHILE PEPPERS

Fresh chile peppers need to be used judiciously. They warm the mouth while adding their own flavor but the heat should not overpower the taste buds. The heat of chile peppers is concentrated in the seeds and interior membrane; careful handling is important.

Long, skinny Thai bird chiles; short and plump serranos; fleshy jalapeños; and inch-long Hawaiian chile peppers are some of the fresh chiles I use. They add color as well as textural crunch. I don't use the very fiery habanero much; if I do, I make a jellylike concoction of sugar, vinegar, water, and habaneros that is cooked until thick like honey and blended to a smooth purée. The initial sweet sensation plays a trick on the palate as the heat sets in.

Fresh chiles last a few days in the refrigerator; for longer storage, freeze them in a plastic bag and remove as needed.

Jalapeño

Serrano

Thai bird

CHILE SAUCES

There is a wide variety of prepared, bottled chile sauces from Asia that offer heat and flavor nuances in marinades, sauces, and dressings and as condiments.

Sriracha, from Thailand, is a good all-purpose chile sauce, a bright red mixture in a clear plastic squeeze bottle with a green top. It is puréed chile peppers with tomato, salt, garlic, vinegar, and sugar that squeezes out like ketchup and packs straightforward heat.

Sambal oelek is an Indonesian chile sauce, another all-purpose one. It is a loose purée of chiles with their seeds, flavored with vinegar and garlic, that comprises a slightly sour and quite hot bright red mixture. I use this interchangeably with *sriracha.*

Chile sauce with garlic is a Chinese sauce, rather thin and lumpy with a salty note. It is used as an ingredient in sauces rather than as a condiment. I generally prefer the Lanchi brand. Because of its saltiness, it's a good idea to mix this in at the beginning of a recipe because you will probably have to adjust for salt.

Sweet chile sauce is noticeably sweet and tangy, its heat coming from the chile seeds in this thick and syrupy mix. This sauce is used mainly as a condiment for grilled or fried chicken and seafood in Southeast Asian preparations. I prefer the Lingham brand from Malaysia but there are many others available.

Chile pepper water is a Hawaiian concoction; my version starts with a good quantity of Hawaiian chile peppers, a pinch of garlic and ginger, salt, and water. The mixture is boiled then puréed in a blender, resulting in a bright red, strong-flavored seasoning. This mixture should be stored in the refrigerator.

Ko chu jang is a Korean chile paste that is based on *dwen jang* (Korean miso), glutinous rice, and ground chile peppers. It can range from salty to sweet and from very hot to pleasantly flavorful. Use it in marinades, sauces, and dressings.

CURRY POWDERS AND PASTES

It's important to draw a distinction between the curries of India and those of Thailand, all of which can be spicy hot since they include chile peppers in some form. Indian curries are seasoned with powdered ground spices and are usually yellow in color due to the inclusion of dried ground turmeric. Curry powders can be mild or hot and their flavor can vary according to the blend of spices.

Thai curries are flavored by pastes of fresh herbs and some ground spices; green is the hottest, followed by red, then yellow, each with different components blended together. *Massaman* curry paste is a Thai paste that includes many spices among the fresh herbs, resulting in a mild but fragrant curry reminiscent of an Indian curry.

Always use curry pastes with coconut milk to temper the saltiness and heat with its inherent sweetness and richness. Prepared pastes are readily available in Asian stores and easy to use: a spoonful or two is all you need to flavor a curry for four servings. Curry pastes will last indefinitely if stored in the refrigerator covered with a thin film of oil.

PEPPERCORNS

Peppercorns lend an assertive flavor and heat that is best paired with robust foods like beef, duck, or tuna. Black peppercorns are the strongest in flavor, picked just before they are fully ripe and dried until they shrivel. A crust of coarsely ground peppercorns will be pungent and gutsy; a fine or medium grind is better when pepper is employed as a seasoning. I like to infuse sauces such as Spicy Mango Sauce (page 133) and Honey Sauce (page 106) with the flavor and spiciness of cracked peppercorns.

White peppercorns come from ripe peppercorn berries whose skins are removed before drying. They have substantial heat and add a distinctive flavor dimension to a dish. Fresh green peppercorns just off the vine are hot with an herbal zestiness; they are usually picked when they are still soft and preserved in salt or brine where their flavor becomes more pungent.

Black, white, and green peppercorns from Ponape in Micronesia are especially good for their zestiness. When I can get them, I use the black ones as a crust in the Ponape Pepper-Crusted Shutome (page 114).

SHICHIMI

Shichimi togarashi—referred to as *shichimi*—is a powdered blend of seven spices used for its intriguing heat in marinades and dressings. This condiment of the Japanese table always includes chile peppers; blends may include poppy seeds, sesame seeds, rapeseeds, mustard seeds, pepper leaf, and dried orange or lemon peel. *Sansho,* a pod of the prickly ash tree, is often included too, lending a tangy, aromatic note to the mix. *Shichimi* is used as a table condiment for noodle dishes and grilled meats and fish, sprinkled on to add a little heat. I like it as a coating and seasoning for fish, chicken, and pork because it browns nicely and forms a crust when seared. *Shichimi* is readily available in Japanese food stores and some supermarkets. It comes in a shaker-style bottle and keeps indefinitely in the pantry.

WASABI

Japanese horseradish, wasabi, is a gnarly root with a lively pale green flesh that I like to use in vinaigrettes, sauces, and condiments for its nose-tingling heat. The pungency of wasabi is appreciated most when served with sashimi and sushi. Wasabi is related to horseradish, which is, in fact, what you get when you purchase "wasabi" in tubes or in dry powdered form. Cultivated in Japan and Oregon, fresh wasabi root is not readily available so the powdered or paste form is often used. Fresh frozen wasabi, available from specialty food suppliers, is the next best choice after fresh.

Oceany

One might first think of fish when considering ocean flavors, but I list here those ingredients used to add a distinctive sea flavor of salty and sweet. Caviars can be used to accent and enhance the taste of a recipe, and I use *konbu* and dashi the way others may use beef or chicken bouillon—as flavor bases.

Since fish and other seafoods have their own distinctive flavors and textures, I don't classify them in this oceany flavor category. You'll find them in the core ingredients section of this pantry.

CAVIARS

Fish roe or caviars add saltiness and their briny flavor to dishes. I like them too, for their bright colors and crunchy or soft textures that add more visual and textural elements to a dish. Find caviars such as *ikura, masago, tarako,* and *tobiko* at Japanese markets, fish markets, or sushi bars; sturgeon caviars can be found at specialty food stores.

True caviar is the roe from sturgeon. Beluga, osetra, and sevruga are the main types, ranging in color from pale silver gray to black, all with a soft texture and briny taste. Sevruga and osetra are not as round in shape as beluga and have a pasty, almost jammy texture that I like; their flavor is more concentrated too.

Crab eggs are bright orange, good for flavoring mousses, soups, and stocks.

Ikura is salmon eggs, red orange, shiny, and about the size of baby peas. Each egg has a firm skin that pops as you bite, releasing the creamy fish oils within.

Masago is smelt roe—tiny, red, and salty.

Tarako is cod roe, a pale pink egg with a mild fish flavor and a creamy, grainy texture. It is sometimes referred to as *mentaiko,* which is actually the deep red roe of Alaskan pollack that is salted and flavored with chile pepper.

Tobiko is the tiny, bright orange egg of the flying fish. The small round eggs are firm and crunchy. *Tobiko* can also be green, flavored with wasabi.

Ikura

Masago

Tobiko   *Tarako*

Konbu

Ogo

Nori

SEAWEEDS

There are a number of seaweeds or sea vegetables, known in Hawaii as *limu,* with a distinctive, briny note that contributes to the depth and rounding of flavor in a dish. Seaweed can be bright green, red, or brown; some are crunchy, soft, or chewy. Seaweed is a good source of protein and complex carbohydrates and is low in calories.

Furikake is one of Japan's best inventions. It is a topping made of bits of seaweed, sesame seeds, fish, and salt that is usually sprinkled over rice. The combination of flavors is terrific and needless to say it's not used on rice exclusively. *Furikake* can be used to coat fish, poultry, and meats; it's a great flavor enhancer that adds an immediate dimension to food.

Konbu has a lot of sweet, ocean flavor. These sheets of seaweed or sea kelp grow in cold water off the coast of northern Japan and the dried sheets are used to make dashi, the basic soup stock in Japanese cuisine. Good quality *konbu* is dark green in color with a white layer of salt; wipe but don't wash the salt off before use. *Konbu* expands as it cooks; it can be used in stewed dishes or eaten fried and salted. It is also used for flavor in pickles and in the making of sushi rice.

Toasted sushi nori has a mild flavor though most people think it will be strong when they see this greenish black sheet wrapped around rice as sushi. One of my favorite ways to use nori is as a crust for cooked fish where it accentuates the fish's oceany flavor. You do have to be careful with nori; if it sits in soup it becomes soft but if it gets moist at room temperature, it becomes chewy. Cut nori into fine strips with a pair of scissors (it's more difficult with a knife) for a visually striking garnish.

Ogo is the name for a crunchy, brown, hairlike seaweed gathered along the shores of Hawaii's beaches or raised on aquaculture farms. It can be eaten in its natural state or blanched in hot water. *Ogo* is often used to add flavor to raw fish and steamed seafood presentations, dressed as a salad or as a garnish. When deep-fried, *ogo* has a hairy, stringlike appearance that is actually beautiful.

Herbs and Spices

Each of these ingredients has its own unique, pungent taste that generally defies placement in the six flavor categories of salty, sweet, sour, bitter, hot, and oceany. I think of herbs and spices as flavor enhancers that can accent other flavors in a recipe. The taste of the herb or spice shouldn't dominate. I list here those herbs and spices that I use most often in my cooking.

BASIL

Basil is a member of the mint family; I mostly use sweet basil and Thai basil. The large green leaves of sweet basil pair well with cream in a sauce, with olive oil for pesto preparations, and most definitely with ripe tomatoes. Purple-stemmed Thai basil is more potent with a sharper edge; I like it in soup, cooked dishes, and Thai-style curries. I like both basils in salads, left whole so you can bite into it and really taste its aniselike quality.

Look for perky, bright-colored leaves when purchasing basil of all kinds. Store for a day or two on your kitchen counter with the stems in water. Fresh basil should be used soon after purchase since moisture and age will turn the leaves dark.

Generally, I use basil cut into julienne strips, or chiffonade. To do this, remove the leaves from the stem, stack individual leaves on top of each other, and roll into a cylinder. Using a very sharp knife—a dull knife will bruise the leaves—gently slice the basil into thin strips.

Purple *shiso*

Ginger

Green *shiso*

Lemon grass

Kaffir lime leaves

CHERVIL

Chervil is a lacy, delicate green I use as a garnish for its refreshing flavor with that hint of anise. Chervil salad with extra virgin olive oil, lemon, salt, and pepper is one of my favorite things. I also use *mitsuba* or trefoil, a Japanese chervil with a mild flavor, in soups.

CILANTRO

Cilantro, also known as coriander leaf or Chinese parsley, is a pungent flat-leafed herb used extensively in Asia (except Japan), India, the Middle East, Africa, and Latin America. It can cut through rich preparations and provide spark to a dish, but for many people it can be an acquired taste. I use cilantro mostly when I'm cooking in the Asian style, not in an American dish, because of its strong flavor.

Cilantro is best when chopped and used fresh; when it is cooked, it turns brown and the flavor becomes grassy and more potent. While I use mostly the leaves picked off the stems, the stems and roots can be used to add flavor to marinades or sauces that will be strained. Look for perky leaves and store cilantro in the refrigerator in a plastic bag, rinsed and dried well, or stand the roots in water and cover with a plastic bag.

GARLIC AND ITS COUSINS

Garlic and ginger are like salt and pepper to me—the foundations of flavor in sauces, marinades, and dressings.

Garlic, the stinking rose, is an important part of the cuisines of China, Korea, and Southeast Asia. A member of the lily family, garlic's aromatic and distinctive pungency set it apart from its relatives—onions, leeks, chives, green onions, and shallots. But the intensity of flavor varies too: white garlic is considered the strongest; the purplish varieties are somewhat milder.

Raw garlic is very pungent so I prefer to mellow it through cooking, especially if I am using it in an uncooked preparation like a salad dressing. I like to have Sautéed Garlic and Garlic Oil (page 151) prepared ahead of time, keeping in mind that it's important not to burn garlic because it will turn bitter.

Garlic should be stored in a cool place but not in the refrigerator. Never store raw garlic cloves in oil. A medium-sized clove, minced, equals about 1 teaspoon.

Green onions, chives, and shallots are also important ingredients in my pantry. Green onions are sometimes referred to as scallions or spring onion. The hollow, long, dark green leaves and white stems of this mild-flavored onion are used as a seasoning, condiment, and garnish. Because they cook quickly and overcooking can cause them to turn bitter, green onions are usually added at the last moment. Finely minced and used raw, green onions enhance flavor, especially in mousses, and their lively green color adds sparkle too. Look for crisp leaves and white stems; store in a plastic bag in the refrigerator for up to a week.

Chives are slender, green onion-like hollow stems with a mild onion flavor. Sliced very fine, I like to add them to soups and sauces, especially butter-based sauces. They make a terrific garnish and pair well with caviar or any type of fish roe. If I can find it, I like to use the thin, miniature Japanese chive known as *meneji.*

I'm a big fan of shallots and use them a lot in my cooking. I like the texture of a shallot: it minces up fine and it has a nice bite to it when it is cooked, compared to onions that get soft. Plus, it has a better flavor than an onion, especially in dressings where onions can be bitter.

I insist on cutting shallots in a perfect square mince: their light purple color sparkles like diamonds in a salad dressing. Also, when you cut a shallot by hand, the aroma is milder than if you pulverize it in a food processor. For some preparations, like a sauce, you may want that stronger flavor and aroma, but for texture in a sauce or vinaigrette, cut it by hand.

Keep a supply of Sautéed Shallots and Shallot Oil (page 153) on hand for some of my recipes.

GINGER AND ITS COUSINS

Ginger is a prized Hawaiian product, grown mostly on the eastern side of the island of Hawaii where rainfall is plentiful and the soil is fertile. An underground creeping rhizome, the knobby hands are harvested between November and March each year, but younger hands are pulled from the earth when the flesh is juicy and crisp to be prepared as *gari* or pickled ginger. As ginger matures, its spicy, medicinal flavor becomes more pungent and its flesh becomes fibrous.

Ginger can be used in chunks, sliced, cut into thin julienne, minced, or grated. Unless it is being used in a preparation where it will be removed from a dish, ginger should be peeled. A simple way to do this is to scrape the skin off with the edge of a spoon.

Pure ginger juice is ideal in dipping sauces when you want concentrated flavor without the fiber. To obtain ginger juice, mince or grate ginger and squeeze in your hand; placing the ginger in cheesecloth can make it easier. Or, use a bamboo or porcelain ginger grater that extracts the juice, leaving the fiber of mature ginger behind.

In Chinese cookery, fish is always paired with ginger to take away any hint of fishiness. Strong-flavored meats, like lamb, are often cooked with ginger to subdue their flavor. Ginger is always used in balance with garlic, refreshing the garlic while garlic softens the medicinal notes of the ginger.

Like garlic, if you are using minced ginger in a salad dressing or other uncooked preparation, it's a good idea to cook it first in oil to take away the pungency. Sautéed Ginger and Ginger Oil (page 151) can be prepared ahead of time and stored in the refrigerator.

Ginger can be stored at room temperature for several days. For longer storage, wrap it in paper towels, place it in a plastic bag, and store in the refrigerator. A quarter-sized slice of ginger about ¼ inch thick will yield about 1 teaspoon of minced ginger.

Myoga is another member of the ginger family that I sometimes use. Prized for its pink-tinged buds with a hot but herbal flavor, it can be sliced thin and eaten raw in salads, with sashimi, or pickled in vinegar to use as a garnish. I especially like to sauté it and use it as a garnish.

Galangal, another form of ginger, is used extensively in Southeast Asia in place of ginger. When I use it, I take into account its more assertive herbal flavor and heat level that can add zest to dishes.

GREEN TEA

Tea is a warm-weather evergreen. How the leaves are processed and their exposure to oxygen determines the three types of tea: black, oolong, and green. Black tea leaves are withered, fermented, and dried, resulting in dark-colored leaves and a hearty-flavored brew. Oolong is only partially fermented so the leaves remain lighter as does the brew. Green tea leaves are simply steamed and dried, producing a light green brew with a slightly bitter but delicate fresh, green taste. Green tea is the preferred beverage in Japan and is used to flavor foods like ice cream and confections.

KAFFIR LIME LEAVES

The dark green leaves of the sour, knobby-skinned kaffir lime are prized for their aroma and the citrusy quality that they impart to soups, marinades, sauces, and curries. Kaffir lime leaves are the Southeast Asian equivalent of the bay leaf, but they can also be sliced thin and used in vinaigrettes and salads where their lemon-lime pungency adds a lively accent. The leaves are available fresh, dried, and in powdered form; fresh leaves can be stored in the freezer.

LEMON GRASS

I first encountered lemon grass when I worked with a cook whose wife was Thai. She got me hooked on this tropical grass. Its herbal flavor can be infused into steaming liquids, its lemony essence forms a nice coating on fish or meats, and it is a key underlying element in Thai-style sauces.

When I'm making a sauce, I use the whole stalk, including the gray-green leaves, and I smash the fibrous end. But when I want to make a dressing or crust fish or steak with lemon grass, I take away the hard outer leaves and use the bottom 6 inches of the bulbous end. I find that mincing lemon grass very fine by hand is preferable to chopping it in a blender, which leaves it stringy.

Lemon grass is available fresh in Southeast Asian grocery stores; it is also available shredded and dried. Fresh stalks will keep in the refrigerator for weeks or you can chop and freeze them.

SHISO

Shiso, also known as perilla or beefsteak leaf, is a heart-shaped, serrated leaf that is a member of the mint family. Its herbal flavor is reminiscent of ginger, basil, and mint and there's a hint of a spicy kick. Green *shiso* is often served with sashimi and sushi and battered for tempura. Red leaves are used in pickling, giving off their color.

Shiso is best when raw and fresh, especially with seafood and shellfish or torn in a salad. When you cook *shiso,* it loses its potency and actually becomes indistinguishable unless you use a lot of it. I like to crust or wrap a piece of fish with *shiso;* it pairs well with soy sauce. *Shiso* buds are strong flavored too; I use them as a flavor accent and garnish. Fresh leaves will last in the refrigerator for up to 5 days.

Core Ingredients

A great meal begins with great ingredients. In cooking, putting the ingredients together so they taste good is only part of the process. The art of cuisine actually begins much earlier, on the farm and in the fields. I have great respect for farmers—it is hard work and a risky business that is often challenged by weather and pests. My television series, *Hawaii Cooks,* has always tried to give audiences a sense of the whole process of cooking from the field to the table, which is what I enjoy most about doing the show.

Part of cooking is respecting and appreciating the raw ingredients. Selecting the right products, the freshest produce, the sweetest fruits, or the most tender cuts of beef is just as vital to cooking as preparing the recipe. Here is a sampling of the core ingredients used most often in my kitchen.

Fish and Seafood

My style of cooking is heavily influenced by both Japan and Hawaii. Having spent so much time on two islands, it's not surprising that I love the challenge of cooking with seafood. There are so many different varieties of seafood, from the sweetness of Kona crab to the meaty texture and flavor of yellowfin ahi, that I'm constantly inspired as a chef.

AHI

Ahi is tuna and in Hawaii it refers to bigeye and yellowfin varieties caught by longline fishermen. The best ahi has good fat content, a nice red color, and is beeflike in texture and taste. The soft-textured red flesh becomes firm and beige when cooked.

In Hawaii, we are big fans of ahi as sashimi , sliced raw fish simply dipped in soy sauce or another condiment. We also relish *poke,* a dish of cubed ahi usually seasoned with soy sauce, garlic, ginger, sesame oil, and green onion—all the flavors I love.

AKU

Aku is skipjack tuna, smaller in size, deeper red in color, and stronger in flavor than ahi. It is often served raw or fried; it takes well to strong seasonings so it is often prepared as *poke*.

KAUAI SHRIMP

Aquaculture farms in Hawaii provide lots of fresh shrimp and prawns for local consumption. Kauai shrimp is one such product, a farm-raised salt-water shrimp with a sweet and crunchy tail. They are available fresh and frozen and are comparable to a Mexican-type shrimp.

KONA COLD LOBSTER

A Kona cold lobster is simply a Maine lobster kept fresh, alive, cold, and happy in waters near Kona at Keahole Point on the island of Hawaii. Here, at the Natural Energy Laboratory, cold nutrient-rich water from depths of three thousand feet is pumped to the surface and used for aquacultured products. After their long journey across the United States, live Maine lobsters are revived in this water before being shipped to restaurants and consumers throughout the Pacific.

KONA CRAB

Kona crab is a bright orange, hard-shelled crab with short legs and average-sized claws protruding from its squarish body. Generally running 1¹/₂ to 2 pounds, it is a long-backed crab found in the waters around Hawaii where it burrows in the sand, hence its tough shell. Most of the meat, sweet and soft, is found in the body, though some will argue that the best meat is in its pincers. The fishing season for this crab is September to April. It's delicious, especially in crab cakes.

TAMASHIRO MARKET

Tamashiro Market is a haven for fish and seafood lovers in Honolulu. Established by the Tamashiro family a half century ago, this store has a fine reputation for a wide variety of fish and seafood from every corner of the world, and especially the freshest selection of fish from island waters. *Poke,* bite-sized morsels of seasoned fish and seafood, is a Tamashiro specialty. More than two dozen kinds of *poke* are featured each day, well seasoned to satisfy discriminating taste buds. Catering to connoisseurs of fine seafood as well as the ethnic neighborhood in which it is located, Tamashiro's is a must-stop for those who love good food.

MAHIMAHI

Mahimahi is the dolphin fish, and it is prized for its firm, white flesh that remains moist and flaky when cooked. It has a hint of sweetness and can be cooked in many ways. Fish usually range from 15 to 25 pounds and are caught in the open ocean.

MEMPACHI

Mempachi is soldier fish, about ¹/₂ to 1 pound in size. Found along Hawaii's shorelines, it is red in color and is well liked for its white, soft, flaky flesh and mild flavor.

MULLET

Mullet is a long-bodied small fish, usually 1¹/₂ to 2 pounds in weight. They are prized for their oily flesh, which pairs well with robust seasonings. Mullet are widely available but can be substituted with any fatty white-fleshed fish.

OPAKAPAKA

Opakapaka is a pink snapper found in the depths of Hawaiian waters. Its flesh is moist and mild flavored with a delicate texture. It is often prepared whole, steamed Chinese-style, and paired with other seafood like scallops, shrimp, and crab. Substitute with black cod, flounder, halibut, ocean perch, rock cod, sole, or turbot.

SHUTOME

Shutome is Hawaiian or broadbill swordfish, caught in the open ocean by longliners. These fish can weigh up to several hundred pounds and most of the islands' catch is exported to mainland markets. The pale pinkish flesh is prized for its sweet, mild flavor and its fat content, making it ideal for pan-frying and grilling.

UHU

Uhu is a greenish blue parrot fish that grazes on coral beds surrounding the Hawaiian islands. Its firm, pale pink flesh is moist, sweet, and well suited to steaming.

UNI

Uni is the sexual gland of the spiny sea urchin, a soft golden blob with a sweet nutty taste. It is a delicacy served in sushi bars, strong when raw but tamed when cooked in sauces. It can be bitter but it pairs well with cream and butter over chicken and also with sesame paste and sesame seeds. A sushi bar would be a good source for this item.

Years ago, I watched a French chef use *uni* in a dish with chicken. The idea stuck with me and later I began experimenting with *uni,* puréeing it so that it became a binding agent in a sauce, adding a velvety dimension.

Vegetables

Vegetables are so versatile. Depending on how you prepare and season them, they can be a refreshing palate cleanser when just lightly seasoned with salt and pepper or they can be a meal in themselves when heavily flavored. Vegetables can also bring textural and flavor balances to a recipe.

ARTICHOKES

An artichoke is the edible flower bud of a thistle plant. I was in culinary school when first I came face-to-face with an artichoke. I started by chewing on the tough outer leaves and then switched to a knife and fork to try to eat it. Obviously, as time passed, I learned how to better deal with this delicacy.

ARUGULA

Also is known as rocket, arugula is a peppery salad green that is a member of the mustard family.

BOK CHOY

Baby bok choy is a jade-hued Chinese cabbage, harvested at about 6 inches tall. It is also known as Shanghai bok choy. Trim the stems and rinse them well but leave the head whole to cook.

BROCCOLINI

Broccolini is a relatively new vegetable, a hybrid of *gai lan* (Chinese broccoli) and broccoli. The stalks are about 6 inches long and fully edible, topped with a broccoli-like head. I like the bright green color and tender but crunchy texture.

CHOY SUM

Choy sum is a bright leafy green with yellow flowers and grooved stems. It is also known as Chinese flowering cabbage and its name means "vegetable hearts." Among Chinese greens, this is considered the best for crunch and taste.

CORN SPROUTS

Bright yellow young shoots of the corn plant, corn sprouts are grown to be used as a garnish. They measure 5 to 6 inches long and have a sweet, definitive corn flavor.

DAIKON

Japanese white radish, daikon is about 6 inches long and 3 inches in diameter. It is crisp and juicy with a hint of heat.

EDAMAME

Edamame are fresh soybeans, wonderful as a snack or included alongside vegetables. They are protein rich and have a lovely soft, apple-green color. Buy them fresh in the pod at farmers' markets, or frozen in the pod or shelled at supermarkets.

HARICOTS VERTS

Haricots verts are young, thin French green beans, about 3 to 4 inches long, with a crunchy texture and concentrated flavor.

KAIWARE

Kaiware is a soft, spicy Japanese radish sprout with a light green stem and small leafy green top.

MAUI ONIONS

Maui onions are grown on the slopes of Mount Haleakala on the island of Maui. Sweet and crunchy, these onions are comparable to Texas Sweets, Vidalias, or Walla Wallas, except we think Maui onions are sweeter because they gain their sugariness under the warm Hawaiian sunshine. Maui onions can be enjoyed raw or cooked and you'll find pickled Maui onions in supermarkets.

MESCLUN

A mixture of tender young greens, mesclun is used as an underlying salad or garnish for many dishes. I prefer the soft rather than crisp mesclun mixtures, with spicy and colorful elements. One such mix known as Nalo Greens comes from farmer Dean Okimoto.

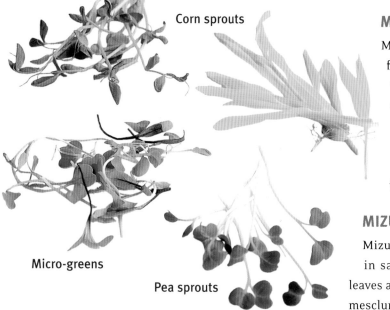

Kaiware

Corn sprouts

Micro-greens

Pea sprouts

MICRO-GREENS

Micro-greens are young shoots of spicy and colorful lettuces that are harvested just days after they sprout. Surprisingly, they have an abundance of flavor; full grown they become part of a tasty mesclun for salads and garnishes, also known as baby greens. In Hawaii, we rely on a spicy mix of micro-greens and mesclun from Nalo Farms in Waimanalo, Oahu.

MIZUNA

Mizuna is a delicate green from Japan that is used in salads and soups. It has feathery dark green leaves and a white stalk and is often picked young for mesclun mixtures.

MUSHROOMS

The musty character of fungi adds a depth of flavor and savoriness to dishes in a pleasant, earthy way.

I use a lot of button mushrooms sautéed with garlic, white wine, and lemon juice in a classic cream sauce. I like Asian mushrooms like shiitake and oyster, grilled whole with salt and pepper and garlic. Fresh shiitake mushrooms contribute a mild woodsy flavor and soft texture to stir-fry dishes; oyster mushrooms have a "fishy" aroma and nuance. For heartiness and chewier textures, use dried shiitake mushrooms; I like to soak them in water overnight and sometimes I use just the water in a preparation.

Dried cèpes and morels have more flavor than fresh ones and are very good in a classic cream, shallot, and white wine sauce. Sometimes I soak these dried mushrooms for 2 to 3 days, reduce the soaking liquid, and use it in a sauce for more concentrated flavor.

Dried Chinese black mushrooms or wood ear mushrooms have their own mild earthy flavor but add crisp, textural crunch as an ingredient in spring rolls and stir-fry dishes.

All dried mushrooms should be reconstituted in water; soak them for as little as 30 minutes in boiling water or up to a few days in tepid water. The soaking liquid can be used in sauces but remember to strain it.

Mild-flavored enoki mushrooms are best raw, tossed in a salad or as a garnish. When they are cooked in a soup or sauce they melt away; tempura batter is a good way to cook them and keep them from wilting.

Matsutakes, steamed or grilled, are full bodied with a chewy texture; when you sauté them in unsalted butter, the flavor is emphasized even more.

Portobello are good whole and grilled, chunky in form, but I don't think they have much flavor as a sauce ingredient. I do like to remove the gills because they turn black when cooked. The gills can be dried out in a low temperature oven and ground up in a blender to make mushroom dust for coating other foods.

NALO FARMS

Dean Okimoto is a close friend and my personal farmer. Years ago when I had just opened the first Roy's Restaurant in East Honolulu, Dean began growing herbs and mesclun for me. Today, he supplies restaurants with the freshest, best-tasting greens and herbs. Dean is a second-generation farmer in the dry, hot Waimanalo Valley on Oahu. We often collaborate on crops: I sometimes bring Dean seeds gathered from my travels or go through seed catalogs with him. He's always experimenting for me, and if he can grow it successfully, he supplies my restaurants. Dean's Nalo Greens is a spicy, soft mixture of arugula, mizuna, red mustard, red oak lettuce, red and green romaine lettuce, curly cress, lollo rossa, redina, red Russian kale, chervil, and French sorrel. It is always served in my Hawaii Kai restaurant and is a well-known product in specialty markets and fine restaurants throughout Oahu.

MUSTARD GREENS

Mustard greens are an all-green, leafy vegetable appreciated for the crunchy, slightly bitter rib section. The paler the color, the more tender the leaves and ribs.

RADICCHIO

Radicchio is red-leafed Italian chicory. I like the slight bitterness of this firm leaf that can be lightly sautéed or grilled and still be crunchy.

SNAP PEAS

Snap peas or sugar snap peas are sweet, crunchy, bright green pea pods that are completely edible. They are slightly plump and should be eaten raw or just slightly cooked so they remain crisp.

Snow peas are another fully edible pea pod, flatter than a snap pea with smaller seeds. These are also known as Chinese snow peas and can be eaten raw or barely cooked for optimum crunch.

GREEN GROWERS FARM

For over half a century, Graf Shintaku has been growing tomatoes hydroponically in Hauula on the north shore of Oahu. When he started, hydroponics was in its infancy and now, amazingly, the same system of feeding nutrients to tomato plants in still in place. Within the one-acre farm, seedlings are planted in black sand in hollow tile beds. Each day, the plants are flushed with water and nutrients while they bask in the open air and warm Hawaiian sun. Picked vine-ripe, these tomatoes are juicy and flavorful, just what a chef likes to serve his customers. Hauula tomatoes are sold under the Green Growers label to restaurants and markets on Oahu throughout the year.

TOMATOES

Every chef covets tomatoes, especially vine-ripened ones. Bursting with flavor and juices, a good tomato can make a dish exceptional. In Hawaii, we are fortunate to have many growers who produce tomatoes all year long, taking advantage of the warm sunny climate that helps to develop great flavor. Long-ignored varieties like the heirloom zebra, green-striped and sweet, are becoming more available.

WARABI

Warabi is a bracken fern shoot, similar to a fiddle-head fern. Also known as *pohole* in Hawaii, it tastes like asparagus, artichoke, and green beans with the earthiness of a mushroom.

WATERCRESS

A member of the mustard family, watercress is full of flavor and spice. Its dark green leaves and slightly bitter flavor are nice additions to salads and stir-fry dishes. As its name suggests, watercress is grown in watery fields and in Hawaii it is available throughout the year.

WON BOK

Won bok is Chinese cabbage, also known as celery cabbage or napa cabbage. The large leaves are light green with white stems, crisp, and mild flavored. Used raw in a salad, won bok does not wilt easily when dressed.

YARD-LONG BEANS

Also known as Chinese long beans, they are a type of green bean that grows up to a yard long, hence the name. Related to the black-eyed pea and similar in flavor to a green bean but without the crisp texture, they are excellent in stir-fries.

Tofu

Tofu is really a category on its own. Also known as soybean curd or soy cheese, it is a protein-rich food with a bland, slightly beany flavor, making it an ideal sponge for sauces and seasonings. Tofu ranges in texture from silky, soft, and fragile to firm and dense. It is an important part of my pantry for its textural quality and its ability to blend with seasonings.

Tofu is made from soybeans that are soaked, cooked, puréed, and mixed with water then pasteurized and mixed with a coagulant to form curds. As in cheese making, liquid is pressed from blocks of curds to form the end product.

In my restaurants, I use firm tofu served as a vegetable, deep-fried or seared. Deep-frying turns tofu golden brown and gives it a chewy texture. Once deep-fried, tofu is also easier to handle; it breaks apart easily uncooked.

Personally, I prefer the soft variety of silky and rich tofu. I especially like it cold, drizzled with a little soy sauce. Soft tofu blends well with ground shrimp or chicken, creating a mousselike mixture that can be fried or steamed. *Yuba,* sturdy sheets of tofu skin formed during tofu making, is an ideal wrapper for this kind of preparation.

Fresh tofu blocks are packaged in water, which should be changed daily to allow for several days of storage in the refrigerator. Tofu should be drained before use, especially when it will be fried. To do this, remove the tofu from its package and position a plate on top of the tofu. Place a weight on the plate and allow it to sit for 15 to 30 minutes. Drain and pat the tofu dry with paper towels, pressing gently to extract moisture.

If you are pan-frying tofu with a minimal amount of oil, always use a nonstick pan. Keep the heat on high and allow time for the tofu to become golden brown and firm. Before deep-frying tofu, it's important to extract as much moisture as possible. As it fries, any moisture will be released into the oil and it will take longer for the tofu to brown and develop a nice firm exterior.

Starches

Grains such as rice and root vegetables such as taro are essential elements of Asian and Pacific cooking. These starches offer a wide variety of preparation possibilities. For example, rice ranges in color from bright white to deep black, and can be made into everything from noodles and flour to creamy milk. Besides being the focal point in a meal, starches can also appear in a dish as a wrapper for spring rolls and pan-fried dumplings.

GYOZA WRAPPERS

Gyozas are Japanese half moon–shaped dumplings that are usually pan-fried and steamed. The wheat flour wrappers are round and slightly thick and are sometimes referred to as pot sticker wrappers. Wonton wrappers, a little thinner and square in shape, can be substituted, cut into rounds with a large biscuit cutter.

LUMPIA WRAPPERS

Lumpia are Filipino egg rolls; the wrapper is a thin crepelike skin made of wheat flour, egg, cornstarch, and water. They are usually 6 to 7 inches square and are available fresh or frozen. To prevent defrosted frozen wrappers from tearing as you pull them apart, divide the stack of wrappers into several smaller stacks, and then peel off single wrappers.

MUNG BEAN NOODLES

Mung bean noodles are also known as bean thread, glass, or cellophane noodles. In their dry form, these bundled noodles are wiry and tough. Soak them in water and they become translucent and slippery. Cook them (page 152) and they become slippery but a little chewy, and they absorb the seasonings in which they are cooked. If you deep-fry them when dry, they turn white, wiry, and crisp.

NOODLES

Noodles are one of my comfort foods. I like them thick and thin, soft and chewy, prepared in a bowl of steaming broth, or pan-fried crisp. There are so many different kinds of noodles and I use them each in their own way.

Udon is a Japanese wheat noodle, white, thick, and chewy, usually served in broth but sometimes stir-fried. *Saimin* is a thinner beige noodle, equivalent to ramen noodles. In Hawaii, these noodles are readily available fresh in supermarkets; elsewhere look for them in Japanese or Asian markets.

OKINAWAN SWEET POTATOES

Purple or Okinawan sweet potatoes are a Hawaiian-grown favorite, deeply hued and sugary sweet. Grown mostly on the island of Molokai, purple sweet potatoes are enjoyed simply baked or steamed, mashed like regular potatoes, diced in salads, battered and fried as tempura, sliced thin and fried as chips, and even in pies and cheesecakes. These sweet potatoes are prized for their firm texture, pleasant sweetness, and their brilliant color.

PANKO

Panko is Japanese dried unseasoned bread flakes, available in packages. As a coating for food, it fries up crisp and crunchy. It is best to dredge food in flour first, dip it in beaten egg, and then coat it with the *panko.* It's important to fry *panko*-crusted foods in oil that is hot, at least 350°F, to insure that the panko will become crisp and crunchy and form a nice crust to seal moisture in. If the oil is not hot enough the *panko* will absorb the oil, resulting in a greasy piece of food. Thicker pieces of food that have been encrusted with *panko* should be fried first, with the cooking finished in the oven.

POI AND TARO

The staple of the native Hawaiian diet, poi is the grayish-purple paste made from cooked taro root. People unfamiliar with it often push it aside; it is, after all, pretty bland. But I'm stubborn about poi: I've eaten it all my life and like it so I want everyone else to like it too.

THE IWAMOTO NATTO AND NOODLE FACTORY

The Iwamoto Natto and Noodle Factory in Paia has been a Maui institution for fifty years. In fact, the factory supplied their products to my grandfather's store in Kahului, Maui. The Yamashita family, third-generation descendants of the founders, continues to make a fresh thick *saimin* noodle that is chewy and texturally interesting.

Saimin is a Hawaiian dish of noodles and broth topped with bits of *char siu* and green onion. At Maui eateries, the broth is served on the side with the thick *saimin* noodles being tossed with bits of *char siu*, green onion, and bean sprouts, and seasoned with oil and soy sauce. The dish, known as dry *mein*, is found only on Maui.

In our restaurants in Hawaii, we make our own poi every day, mashing the cooked taro to a thick, starchy paste. We don't add water like the commercial poi makers do. We fly poi to our mainland restaurants where it is on all of our menus. We serve it like a sauce, with a spicy salted salmon and tomato relish and braised short ribs.

There are many varieties of taro. Some are used mashed, like a potato, others sliced thin and fried like potato chips. I also use taro leaves because they have an earthy, smoky flavor that is unique. Once cooked (page 156), I sauté the chopped leaves in butter with shallots and garlic. Sometimes I use the cooked leaves in sauces, but instead of making a purée, I like to retain the bite of chopped leaves.

RICE

Rice is one of two starch staples in the islands (the other is poi). Medium-grain Calrose rice is the most popular, white and sticky and served with just about anything at any time of day. Premium short- to medium-grain rice has become more available and popular in the islands; it is sticky, slightly sweet, glossy, and translucent when cooked, and is often referred to as "sushi rice."

In addition to "plain white rice," I like to use an array of rices from Asia. Thai sticky rice is long-grain sweet rice that is best steamed after soaking in water overnight. The grains stick together but are dry and firm compared to short-grain glutinous rice that is moist and sticky and ideal for pounding into a smooth paste for confections.

Long-grain Thai black rice has its colored bran layer intact. It becomes purplish black when cooked and has a nutty flavor and slightly firmer texture. Basmati and jasmine rice are prized for their aroma and their separate long grains.

WASHING AND COOKING RICE

Washing rice before cooking it is a ritual performed by virtually every cook in Hawaii. We rinse the grains in cool water from the tap, scrubbing them a little to release the nutrient-rich talc that has been applied to the polished grains. Yes, we wash away the vitamins and minerals. But it is a habit for all of us who have grown up eating and cooking rice and, in my opinion, the rice tastes "cleaner."

To wash rice, place it in a bowl or your rice pot and cover with water. Swish it around with your fingers, pour off the water, and repeat this process two or three more times until the water is clear. Or, you could put the rice in a fine-meshed sieve and run water over it as you swish it around with your fingers. Whichever way you do it, the water should not be cloudy.

In Hawaii, automatic rice cookers are as common as microwaves in the kitchen. Just put in your measured and washed rice, add water to the proper level, cover, and push the button. Your rice is perfectly cooked 20 to 25 minutes later.

If you do not have a rice cooker, place washed rice and measured water in a covered saucepan. Bring to a boil over high heat. Decrease the heat to low and cook for 15 minutes. Turn off the heat and let the rice stand for 10 to 15 minutes before serving.

Arborio is plump, medium-grain rice that can absorb much more liquid than other rice. It is originally from Italy and is identified by a white dot in the center of the grain. As it cooks with liquid, Arborio rice releases its starch and the grains become chewy while the dish becomes creamy. Look for Arborio rice in supermarkets, specialty food stores, and Italian grocery stores.

Meats

Generally we think of meats as something to be flavored, but I use the meats listed here as flavoring components and accents. *Char siu* brings sweetness, pancetta brings saltiness, and Portuguese sausage adds heat and spice.

CHAR SIU

Char siu is Chinese barbecued pork, sweet-salty from its marinade of honey and fermented black beans. Garlic and Chinese five-spice powder also flavor these pork pieces that are usually hung over a charcoal fire to cook, emerging red, slightly charred, and tender. I like to use *char siu* as a meaty addition to fried rice or stuffing for poultry; its savory sweetness pairs well with vegetables in stir-fry dishes too.

HAWAIIAN MEAT

On the Big Island of Hawaii, cattle roam freely on acres and acres of grasslands, so my restaurant there serves as much of this forage-fed beef as it can. Slightly chewier than commercially fed beef but well flavored, it's a treat to use this island-grown product. But production of this meat, as well as grass-fed lamb, is still limited, so we continue to rely on good outside purveyors for much of our beef and lamb.

PANCETTA

Pancetta is cured pork belly, salted, spiced, and rolled into a cylinder like a jelly roll. This Italian bacon differs from its American counterpart in that it is not smoked and, because it is cured, it can be eaten without cooking. It lends a salty but spicy flavor and the fat it renders is a savory addition to a dish. I use pancetta as a meat component and a salty agent, particularly against the sweetness and acidity of balsamic vinegar in a salad. Pancetta can be found in specialty food shops or Italian delis; store it in the refrigerator, well wrapped, or freeze it for longer storage.

PORTUGUESE SAUSAGE

Portuguese sausage is Hawaii's distinctive sausage, eaten for breakfast with eggs and rice and essential in a hearty bean soup popular in the islands. It is simply chunky, fatty pork seasoned with garlic, salt, vinegar, herbs, and varying amounts of chile pepper. I use Portuguese sausage in rice dishes or when I steam seafood, especially clams. This meat product is widely available in supermarkets in Hawaii; elsewhere, look for *linguisa.*

Ingredients to Add Richness

While it is true that a high-fat diet is not very healthy, fats are an important part of cooking and really add richness and velvety mouth-feel to recipes. As with everything else in cooking, balance is the key—too much fat and a rich and creamy texture can become heavy and unappetizing. If you are going to use fat, make it count by using high-quality butters, creams, and cold-pressed oils. I'm sorry, but most fat substitutes just can't duplicate the texture and richness of the real thing.

BUTTER

Butter and cream enter into my style of cooking from my classical French training, adding richness to foods and coating the mouth for a texturally soothing sensation.

Butter itself is very tasty. If you cook a neutral-tasting fish in butter, it will take on a whole new flavor as the butter browns and becomes nutty. I like to add butter to sauces just before they are served to mellow and round any sharp flavors like the flavor of black beans in the Char Siu Pork Chops (page 100).

I almost always use whole butter rather than clarified butter, which has less flavor because the milk solids are removed. Unsalted butter allows me to control the amount of salt in a dish. When you are using butter for sautéing, heat your pan over medium-high rather than high heat to prevent the butter from burning.

COCONUT MILK

Coconut milk is the thick, sweet liquid strained from grated coconut meat soaked in water; it is not the water found in fresh coconuts. Making fresh coconut milk requires opening a coconut, extracting the meat, peeling the skin, and grating the meat to a fine pulp. The pulp is then soaked in boiling water, then strained. While you can't beat the flavor of fresh coconut milk, I bow to convenience and use canned coconut milk, which is always readily available.

I like to add coconut milk to sauces and marinades, generally with lots of garlic, ginger, and fish sauce; the strong flavors are softened and the creaminess adds richness. In a salad dressing, a little coconut milk can be used for a creamy base and act as an emulsifier. In custardy desserts, coconut milk can replace cream to lend its distinctive flavor and richness.

When using canned coconut milk, shake the can before opening it to blend the coconut cream at the top of the can and the liquid beneath. If a recipe calls for coconut cream, do not shake the can; just spoon off the top layer. Coconut milk is perishable so any leftovers should be refrigerated or frozen. It can curdle during cooking so it's important to stir continuously once it's over heat.

CREAM

Cream adds a velvety texture to sauces, coating the tongue and mouth in richness. Certain sauces, like those with a base of well-flavored stock, require cream to round the flavors, like the Asian-Style Spicy Peppercorn Steak (page 92). I prefer cream with 36 to 38 percent butterfat because it reduces well; with heavier creams, reduction occurs too quickly, before the flavor of a stock has a chance to flavor the cream.

MACADAMIA NUTS AND OIL

Buttery, rich, crunchy Hawaiian macadamia nuts are always in my pantry. Not only are these nuts excellent in desserts, but I also use them to coat fish and meats to provide textural contrast. Chopped macadamia nuts are good in rice dishes and salads, as well. Buy macadamias already chopped, if you can; whole nuts tend to shard when you cut them.

Macadamia nut oil can be definitive or very bland, depending on the manufacturer, so be sure to taste it before using and adjust your other seasonings accordingly. This oil is good for high-temperature cooking since it has a high smoke point.

SESAME SEEDS AND OIL

Sesame seeds have their own unique sweet, nutty flavor. The flat white seeds become more flavorful after toasting in a hot pan (see page 153) and crushing them releases even more of their flavor. Black seeds are visually wonderful as a garnish, even simply sprinkled over white rice.

Roasted and crushed seeds are pressed for their richly flavored oil. As a seasoning, marinade ingredient, and condiment, sesame oil plays an important role in my cooking. It is often drizzled onto a dish just before serving so that its aroma and nuttiness tantalize the senses. Sesame oil is not suited to deep-frying because of its low burning point.

STOCK AND DEMI-GLACE

Stock is the foundation of my sauces, especially reduced stock or demi-glace. It is a long process to make stock but it is not hard. I use beef meat and veal bones for my stocks. Stock made with meat alone is powerful in flavor but it doesn't become gelatinous like stock made from bones. In my restaurant kitchens, the beefy liquid extracted from braising short ribs is combined with veal stock and reduced to make demi-glace, intensely rich and thick.

Flavoring agents in my stockpots include tomatoes, herbs, and *mire-poix* (carrot, celery, onion). We slice the onions thick and burn them until they are black so that the stock takes on some color. You can roast the bones for color but sometimes they will burn and the stock will become bitter. I never add salt to the stock because the salt will become concentrated when you reduce it.

After boiling this mixture for hours and hours to extract the flavors of the ingredients, the liquid is strained and chilled (or frozen). Then the fat is removed and the liquid reduced by simmering for many more hours. Stock becomes demi-glace when it is thick and syrupy; once it is reduced and chilled, it is so thick it can be cut with a knife.

Flavor packed demi-glace is added to sauces to make a dish rich and robust compared to butter sauces that are silkier and finer. Demi-glace can also mellow sharp flavors like red Thai curry paste and make it more wine friendly. When I use demi-glace, I never use salt; the natural flavor of demi-glace is enough to satisfy.

Stocks, of course, are not just about beef and veal; chicken and seafood stocks are important too, depending on what you are making and what the final outcome will be. And there is dashi, the Japanese stock of *konbu* (sea kelp) and *katsuobushi* (bonito flakes) that can add a briny, oceany essence to sauces and dressings. Each stock adds another layer of flavor to whatever is being cooked with it.

Recipes

My recipes can be daunting at first glance: the list of ingredients is often long and there may be two to three preparations for a dish. I realize that in a restaurant kitchen there are prep cooks who have sliced, diced, julienned, and minced the vegetables and herbs and the pantry is well-stocked with all the sauces, flavorings, and fresh ingredients I will need. A home kitchen may not be as all encompassing, but with some smart shopping and organization, my recipes can be successfully duplicated.

Realize that a recipe for a dish is really a complete meal. There is a protein and a side dish of vegetables and/or starch, a sauce, and a garnish in each dish presented. You may want to add an appetizer, salad, or dessert, but essentially you only have to focus on one recipe.

Realize too that a dish can be broken down into separate parts. I have designed the dishes to encompass all the components I feel go well together, but there's nothing wrong with taking, say, the Ponape Pepper-Crusted Shutome (page 114) and serving it with steamed rice and a salad, or the Thai Black Rice Risotto (page 103) and serving it alone. Each part of a dish will be flavorful and can stand on its own.

Be creative. If you don't have one vegetable, another will easily substitute. A firm white fish in your region will substitute well for mahimahi. Remember, it's all about fresh ingredients, especially those grown and harvested close to home. And it's the flavors that you want to play with because that's where the excitement of my cooking is.

Stock your pantry well. There's quite an array of bottled and prepared Asian ingredients that may be unfamiliar to you or that you think you may never use again. But you will use them and these products last a long time. Once they are opened, store them in the refrigerator.

Recipes are meant to be guidelines: you can increase or decrease the quantity of an ingredient used in a dish. Home cooks have tested all of the recipes in this book and the measurements given will replicate their experience. But let your palate be the judge as to the right balance of ingredients for you.

It's important to visually understand a recipe: read through it and go through each item and each step in the cooking process in your mind. Be organized: it's wise to have each ingredient prepared and measured, lined up in small bowls in the order you will use them just like we do on television. This will help immensely in the final steps of preparation.

Last but not least, have fun. Cooking is all about enjoying the process as well as the presentation. For me, cooking is rewarding because I am able to use my mind, my hands, and my taste—all things that have been given to me in life—to create something for which I will be given immediate reward. When I serve food the reaction makes it all worthwhile. It will for you too.

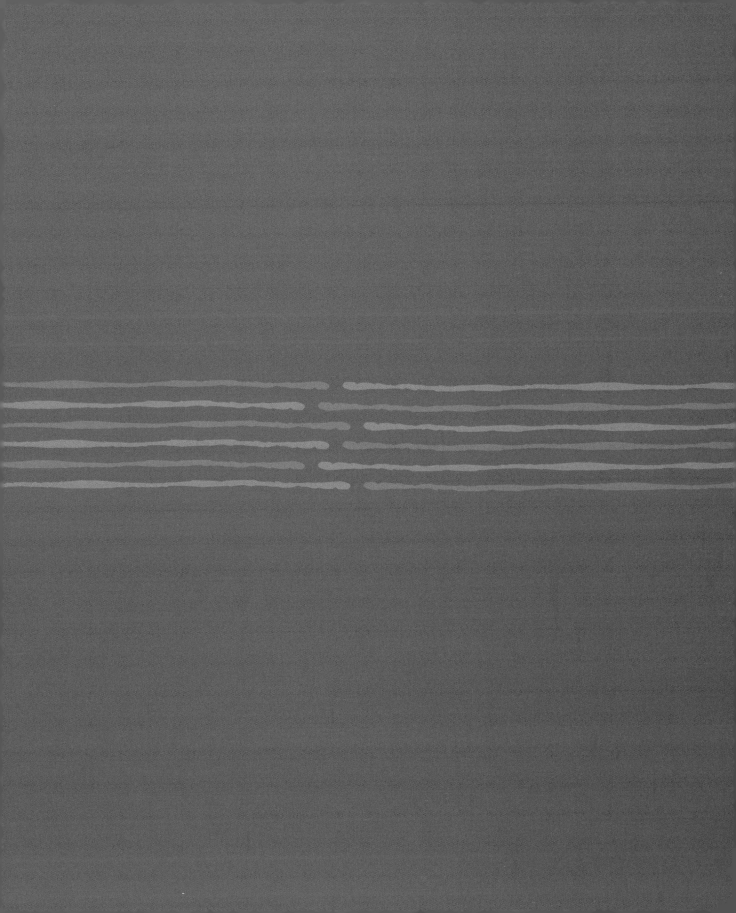

Appetizers, Small Plates, and Cocktails

Wok-Charred Edamame

SERVES 4 TO 6

1 pound edamame in the pod, fresh or frozen

2 tablespoons salt

3 tablespoons sesame oil

2 teaspoons finely minced fresh garlic

1 teaspoon finely minced fresh ginger

1 teaspoon white sesame seeds

1 tablespoon sugar

1 tablespoon soy sauce

1 to 2 teaspoons shichimi (see page 28)

1 teaspoon rayu (see page 25)

1 tablespoon unsalted butter

1 teaspoon rice vinegar

Edamame (soybeans) in their pods are a protein-rich food, popular in Hawaii as a healthy snack food. Chef Ruth Rasmussen of Roy's Restaurants created this dish of stir-fried edamame pods laced with savory Asian seasonings. It's a fun way to eat soybeans because you get all the wonderful flavors in your mouth as you pull out the soybeans from their pods with your teeth.

In a large pot, bring 4 quarts of water to a boil over high heat. Add the edamame and the salt and boil for 8 to 10 minutes, until the beans are tender but not mushy. Drain in a colander.

Heat a large wok over medium-high heat. Add 2 tablespoons of the oil and toss in the edamame. Stir-fry for 1 to 2 minutes, until well coated with the oil.

Make a well in the edamame and add the remaining 1 tablespoon oil, garlic, and ginger. Stir-fry for 20 to 30 seconds, until barely light golden brown, then add the sesame seeds to the well. Stir to mix evenly, coating the edamame. Sprinkle in the sugar and toss several times, allowing the sugar to melt and glaze the edamame. Add the soy sauce, *shichimi,* and *rayu* and mix well. Melt the butter over the edamame, add the vinegar, and mix well. Taste and adjust seasoning with salt if necessary. Transfer to a platter and serve immediately.

Roy's Tips

If you are using fresh edamame, rinse them first to remove any impurities. If you are using frozen edamame, take them directly from the freezer to the boiling water without defrosting.

Don't be alarmed at the amount of salt that goes into the water to cook the edamame; the pods are thick and the salt will not penetrate completely.

If you do not have a wok or sauté pan large enough to hold all the edamame at once, stir-fry in batches so that the pan retains its heat.

To avoid burning garlic and ginger while stir-frying, make a little well in the middle of the ingredients cooking in your pan and add a little oil. Add the garlic and ginger to the well and sauté for 20 to 30 seconds, until barely light golden brown. Then, mix them around to distribute them evenly.

Aku Tataki

SERVES 4 TO 6

SAKE-SOY SAUCE

1/2 cup sake

2 tablespoons soy sauce

1 teaspoon minced fresh garlic

1 teaspoon minced fresh ginger

1 teaspoon sesame seeds

1 pound aku loin

2 Maui or other sweet onions, sliced thin, for garnish

Kesuke "Casey" Asai of Imanas Tei Restaurant in Honolulu was a guest on Hawaii Cooks with Roy Yamaguchi and created "sake magic" in this simple dish. Tataki is a Japanese preparation of tuna in which the outside is seared to seal in the moisture and the inside is raw. Heat mellows the flavor of sake, which smoothes the saltiness of soy sauce in a light but definitive accompaniment for meaty flavored aku (skipjack tuna). Crunchy sweet onions play against the soft texture of the fish in a delightful way.

Heat the sake in a small saucepan over medium-high heat. When the sake is hot, light a match to the sake to burn off the alcohol. When the flame subsides, add the soy sauce, garlic, ginger, and sesame seeds. Decrease the heat to low and simmer for 10 minutes, or until reduced by one-third. Remove the pan from the heat and place in a bowl of ice water to cool.

Trim the *aku*, leaving the skin on. Skewer the *aku* crosswise with 2 metal skewers. Hold the skewers as you sear the *aku* over a gas flame for 30 to 60 seconds, until all sides are seared. Transfer to a bowl of ice water to cool.

Remove the *aku* from the water and pat dry with a kitchen towel. Cut into 3/8-inch slices and arrange on a serving platter. Mound the onions on top of the *aku* and drizzle with the sauce. Serve immediately.

Roy's Tips

Maui onions can be substituted with other sweet onions like Walla Wallas, Texas Sweets, or Vidalias. If you do not have sweet onions, use a yellow cooking onion, slice it thin, and place in a bowl. Run tap water over the onions for 10 to 15 minutes to remove the sharp flavor. Drain well to use.

If you do not have a gas range, sear the aku on all sides in a sauté pan over high heat.

Shrimp on a Sugar Cane Stick with Pineapple-Mango Jam

SERVES 6

PINEAPPLE-MANGO JAM

1 cup finely diced fresh pineapple

1 cup finely diced ripe mango

2 to 3 tablespoons sugar

1 cup sweet white wine or sake

16 shrimp (about $^1/_2$ pound), peeled, deveined, and without tails

4 ounces minced pork with fat, about $^1/_2$ cup

3 strips bacon, minced, about $^1/_3$ cup

4 water chestnuts

$^1/_2$ cup cooked mung bean noodles (page 152)

$^1/_2$ teaspoon salt

2 teaspoons sugar

1 tablespoon fish sauce

1 tablespoon toasted rice powder (page 153)

2 teaspoons garlic oil (page 151)

12 (3 by $^1/_4$-inch) sugar cane sticks (see page 20)

Peanut oil, for deep-frying

Lettuce leaves, for garnish

The smoky, saltiness of bacon and the brininess of shrimp come through in this savory mixture that you bite off a juicy sugar cane stick. Mung bean noodles add a little chewiness and water chestnuts provide crunch; toasted rice powder is the secret to binding the mixture together. A fruity jam provides a light and sweet accompaniment.

To prepare the jam, combine the pineapple, mango, sugar, and wine in a saucepan over high heat. Bring to a boil, decrease the heat to low, and simmer for 30 to 45 minutes, until thick and reduced by half.

To prepare the shrimp, place half of the shrimp in a food processor and chop to a fine mince. Add the remaining shrimp, pork, bacon, water chestnuts, noodles, salt, sugar, fish sauce, rice powder, and garlic oil. Process the mixture until it is pasty but the shrimp is still a little chunky.

Moisten your hands with water and shape about $^1/_4$ cup of the shrimp mixture in a flat mound around the center of a sugar cane stick. Repeat until all the mixture and sugar cane pieces have been used.

Pour oil into a wok to a depth of 3 to 4 inches. Heat the oil over high heat. When the oil is hot, decrease the heat to medium-high and slide in two or three of the shrimp sticks. Fry for 3 to 5 minutes, turning, until golden brown. Transfer to paper towels to drain any excess oil. Repeat with the remaining sticks.

Line a serving platter with the lettuce leaves. Arrange the shrimp sticks on the leaves and serve immediately with the jam alongside.

Roy's Tip

Once you have shaped the shrimp mixture onto the sugar cane sticks, they can be refrigerated, covered, for several hours before frying.

Spicy Chicken Wings

SERVES 6

12 chicken wings

$1/4$ cup cornstarch

2 tablespoons flour

$1^1/2$ tablespoons sugar

1 teaspoon salt

2 tablespoons chopped green onion

1 tablespoon white sesame seeds

2 cloves fresh garlic, chopped

$1/3$ cup soy sauce

1 egg

Canola oil, for deep-frying

DIPPING SAUCE

$2/3$ cup Lingham chile sauce or other
   sweet chile sauce

2 tablespoons soy sauce

2 tablespoons chopped green onion

SALAD

12 asparagus tips

2 cups baby romaine leaves,
   about 18

$1/2$ cup julienned carrot

$1/2$ cup julienned cucumber

$1/2$ cup finely sliced red cabbage

12 slices avocado

1 cup cooked mung bean noodles
   (page 152)

One way to add flavor to fried foods is to season the coating. In this case I've added pungent garlic and salty soy sauce to a thin egg batter. The spicy dipping sauce reinforces the zesty coating, which is balanced by the cool, crunchy vegetables and creamy avocado.

Trim any excess skin off the chicken wings. Cut off and discard the wing tips then cut each wing into 2 pieces at the joint.

In a bowl, combine the cornstarch, flour, sugar, and salt and mix well. Add the green onion, sesame seeds, garlic, soy sauce, and egg and whisk together to form a thin batter. Place the chicken in the batter and mix well to coat. Cover and marinate in the refrigerator for at least 6 hours or preferably overnight, stirring once or twice.

To prepare the dipping sauce, combine all the ingredients in a small bowl and mix well. Cover and refrigerate until ready to use.

To prepare the salad, bring a pot of water to a boil over high heat. Add a little salt and the asparagus. Blanch for about 3 minutes, leaving the asparagus slightly crisp. Drain in a colander and immediately plunge into a bowl of ice water to stop the cooking. Drain again.

To fry the chicken wings, pour oil into a wok to a depth of 3 to 4 inches. Heat the oil over medium-high heat. Stir the chicken, mixing well with the marinade. When the oil is at 325°F, add the chicken in batches and fry for 3 to 4 minutes, until golden brown, crisp, and cooked through. Drain the chicken on paper towels and transfer to a bowl. Add half of the dipping sauce and toss to coat evenly.

To serve, arrange all of the salad ingredients, including the asparagus, on a serving platter. Place the chicken on top of the salad. Drizzle with the remaining sauce or serve it alongside.

Roy's Tip

The frying oil should not be too hot, otherwise the sugar and soy sauce in the coating will burn. In between batches of chicken wings, skim the oil with a fine-meshed skimmer to remove any bits of coating that may be left behind.

Shrimp and Scallop Spring Rolls with Champagne–Caviar Sauce

SERVES 6

2 tablespoons vegetable oil

1 tablespoon sesame oil

1 tablespoon minced fresh garlic

1 tablespoon minced fresh ginger

1^1/$_2$ ounces fresh shiitake mushrooms, chopped, about ^{3}/$_4$ cup

2 cups chopped won bok (napa cabbage)

1 cup cooked mung bean noodles (page 152)

^{1}/$_2$ cup chopped water chestnuts

3 tablespoons fish sauce

^{1}/$_2$ pound medium shrimp, peeled, deveined, and without tails, chopped, about 1 cup

8 large scallops, cut into ^{1}/$_2$-inch chunks, about 1 cup

12 lumpia wrappers

1 egg, beaten

Canola oil, for deep-frying

SAUCE

^{1}/$_2$ cup sour cream

2 tablespoons tobiko, plus additional for garnish (see page 29)

2 tablespoons masago, plus additional for garnish (see page 29)

1 tablespoon freshly squeezed lemon juice

2 tablespoons freshly squeezed orange juice

2 tablespoons Champagne or sparkling wine

Pinch of salt

2 tablespoons finely minced chives, for garnish

Almost every Asian cuisine has a fried roll filled with savory ingredients and dipped in a sauce. In this spring roll, chunky seafood, crunchy water chestnuts, and the crispy wrapper play against a silky, creamy sauce that picks up the briny flavors of the filling.

Heat a sauté pan over high heat. Add the vegetable oil and sesame oil to the pan. When the oils are hot, add the garlic, ginger, and mushrooms and sauté for 20 to 30 seconds, until the garlic is barely light golden brown. Add the won bok, noodles, and water chestnuts and sauté for 1 minute, or until the won bok is wilted. Add 1^1/$_2$ tablespoons of the fish sauce and mix well. Transfer the mixture to a bowl and allow to cool. Drain and squeeze out the excess liquid. Return the mixture to the bowl and add the shrimp, scallops, and the remaining 1^1/$_2$ tablespoons fish sauce, and mix well.

Lay out the lumpia wrappers on a flat surface. Place 2 to 3 tablespoons of the filling in each wrapper. Roll and fold in the sides forming a compact, cigar-shaped spring roll. Brush the open edge with the egg to seal.

To prepare the sauce, combine the sour cream, *tobiko*, *masago*, lemon juice, orange juice, Champagne, and salt in a small bowl and mix well.

In a wok, heat 3 to 4 inches of canola oil over medium-high heat. When the oil is hot, place 3 or 4 spring rolls into the oil and fry for 2 to 3 minutes, until golden brown and crisp. Drain on paper towels. Repeat with the remaining rolls. Transfer to a cutting board and cut in half.

Divide the sauce among 6 plates. Arrange the spring rolls on top of the sauce. Sprinkle with chives and top the spring rolls with *tobiko* and *masago*.

Seafood Full Moon Dumplings with Crispy Ogo

SERVES 6

2 teaspoons vegetable oil

4 fresh shiitake mushrooms, chopped

6 medium shrimp, peeled, deveined, and without tails, chopped

4 large scallops, chopped

4 ounces opakapaka or other mild white fish such as snapper, chopped, about 1/2 cup (see page 38)

2 tablespoons chopped green onion

4 sweet basil leaves, julienned

1 tablespoon sautéed garlic (page 151)

1 tablespoon sautéed ginger (page 151)

1 tablespoon fish sauce

2 tablespoons soy sauce

Salt and freshly ground black pepper

1 tablespoon cornstarch

1/4 cup water

24 gyoza wrappers (see page 47)

SALSA

1 tomato, peeled, seeded, and chopped

1/4 cup chopped ogo (see page 30)

1 teaspoon sautéed garlic (page 151)

1 teaspoon sautéed ginger (page 151)

2 tablespoons chopped onion

1 tablespoon chopped green onion

(continued)

A savory mix of seafood fills these round dumplings accented by oceany flavors in a vibrant salsa and delicate sauce. Crunchy hair-like ogo *is deep-fried for a dramatic contrast to the soft-textured dumplings.*

To prepare the dumplings, heat a small sauté pan over high heat. Add the oil and when it is hot, add the mushrooms and sauté for about 1 minute, or until lightly browned. Transfer to a mixing bowl.

Add the shrimp, scallops, *opakapaka,* green onion, basil, sautéed garlic, and sautéed ginger to the bowl and toss together. Add the fish sauce and soy sauce, season with salt and pepper, and mix well.

In a small bowl, whisk together the cornstarch and water. Place about 1 1/2 tablespoons of the filling in the middle of a wrapper. Moisten the edges of the wrapper with the cornstarch mixture, place another wrapper on top, and pinch the edges to seal. Transfer to a baking sheet, cover, and refrigerate until ready to cook.

To prepare the salsa, mix together the tomato, *ogo,* sautéed garlic, sautéed ginger, onion, and green onion in a small bowl. Season with salt and pepper to taste.

To prepare the sauce, combine the chicken stock, crabmeat, and chives in a small saucepan over medium heat. When the mixture is near boiling, add the butter, a little at a time, whisking to incorporate before adding more. Add salt and pepper to taste. Keep warm.

For the garnish, cut the *ogo* into small clusters and coat with flour. In a saucepan, heat 2 to 3 inches of oil over high heat. When the oil is hot, add the *ogo* in 2 or 3 batches and fry for 30 to 45 seconds, until golden brown and crisp. Transfer the *ogo* to paper towels to drain.

To cook the dumplings, bring a wide saucepan of water to a boil over high heat. Place the dumplings in the water, a few at a time, and cook for 3 to 5 minutes, until the dumplings float to the top of the water. Remove with a slotted spoon and drain well.

Divide the dumplings among 6 plates. Spoon the salsa on top of the dumplings and pour the sauce around. Garnish with crispy *ogo* and serve immediately.

SAUCE

$1/2$ cup chicken stock (page 150)

$1/2$ cup crabmeat, fresh or canned

2 tablespoons chopped chives

$1/4$ cup unsalted butter

1 cup ogo, for garnish (see page 30)

Flour, for dredging

Canola oil, for frying

Roy's Tip

The dumplings can be prepared ahead of time and kept in the refrigerator, covered, for several hours before cooking. They can also be prepared and frozen; take them directly from the freezer to boiling water to cook them.

Molded Sushi with Unagi and Spicy Crab

SERVES 4

SUSHI RICE

2 cups short-grain white rice

5-inch-square piece konbu
(see page 30)

2 cups water

$1/4$ cup rice vinegar

3 tablespoons sugar

1 teaspoon salt

$1/2$ cup mayonnaise

$1^1/2$ tablespoons white miso

2 teaspoons teriyaki sauce (page 154)

1 tablespoon sambal oelek or
sriracha (see page 26)

1 cup cooked crabmeat

12 ounces prepared, cooked
unagi (eel)

Various caviars such as tobiko, ikura,
and black caviar, for garnish

Micro-greens, for garnish

Enoki mushrooms, for garnish

Nori, cut into strips, for garnish

Kabayaki sauce, bottled, for garnish
(see page 17)

This layered sushi molded in a traditional wooden box is typical of southern Japan. The savory unagi *(sea eel) and the rich and creamy crab mixture are a wonderful combination with the vinegary sushi rice.* Kabayaki *sauce, traditionally made with eel bones and soy sauce, provides sweetness. This is a hearty, filling appetizer that could be a meal in itself.*

To prepare the rice, place the rice in a bowl and rinse well. Repeat until the water runs clear. Set the *konbu* in the bottom of a rice cooker. Place the washed rice on top of the *konbu* and add the water. Turn the rice cooker on.

In a small bowl, whisk together the vinegar, sugar, and salt until dissolved.

When the rice cooker turns off, allow the rice to sit for 10 to 15 minutes. Scoop the rice into a bowl (preferably a traditional rice-cooling bowl made of cypress wood); discard the *konbu*. Sprinkle the vinegar mixture over the rice. Mix with a rice paddle or wide wooden spoon while fanning the rice to cool. Taste and adjust the seasoning with vinegar if necessary.

In a bowl, combine the mayonnaise, miso, teriyaki sauce, and *sambal oelek* and mix well. Add the crab and stir well.

Preheat the broiler. To assemble, line a wood sushi mold with plastic wrap, overlapping the edges and sides. In batches, line the mold with rice, press firmly, and top with a layer of *unagi,* then another layer of rice. Press down the rice with the top of the mold so that it is evenly packed.

Unmold the mixture, remove the plastic wrap, and carefully transfer the sushi directly onto a broiler pan. Spoon the crab mixture over the top and place under the broiler for 5 to 10 minutes, until browned. Remove from the broiler and allow to cool for 1 to 2 minutes.

Cut the sushi into serving-sized pieces and arrange on 4 plates. Garnish with caviars, micro-greens, mushrooms, and nori strips and drizzle with *kabayaki* sauce. Serve immediately.

Roy's Tips

In place of the traditional square wood sushi mold, you can use an 8-inch square cake pan, lined with plastic wrap.

Prepared unagi *can be purchased from Japanese markets or sushi bars.*

Crab and Taro Cakes with Béarnaise Sauce

SERVES 4

BÉARNAISE SAUCE

1/2 cup red wine vinegar

1/4 cup chopped fresh tarragon leaves

1 shallot, chopped

1 teaspoon freshly crushed black peppercorns

3 egg yolks

1/4 cup unsalted butter, chilled and cut into pieces

Salt

2 small russet potatoes, boiled and peeled

1/2 cup cooked taro or spinach leaves, chopped (page 156)

1 cup cooked crabmeat

1/4 cup fresh poi (see page 48)

Hawaiian salt and freshly ground black pepper

Flour, for dredging

2 eggs, beaten

1 1/2 cups panko (see page 48)

1/4 cup canola oil

2 tablespoons white vinegar

8 eggs

A crisp cake of potato, crab, and taro, bound together with poi, is the base of this takeoff on eggs Benedict. A zesty sauce balances the richness of the fried cake and the poached egg provides a soft contrast. It's a little different from the classic but every bit as rich and filling for brunch, lunch, or dinner.

To prepare the sauce, combine the vinegar, tarragon, shallot, and peppercorns in a saucepan over medium-high heat and bring to a boil. Decrease the heat to low and simmer for 20 to 25 minutes, until reduced to about 1 tablespoon.

Transfer the vinegar reduction to the top of a double boiler positioned over simmering water. Add the egg yolks and 1 to 2 teaspoons of water and mix with a whisk. Slowly add the butter, whisking to keep the mixture creamy, adding a little water as needed. When all the butter is incorporated, season with salt to taste. Keep the sauce warm.

To prepare the cakes, mash the potatoes in a bowl. Add the taro, crab, and poi and mix well. Season with salt and pepper to taste.

Shape the mixture into 8 small cakes. Coat each cake in the flour, dip in the beaten eggs, and coat in the *panko.*

Heat 2 tablespoons of the oil in a sauté pan and when it is hot, add 4 of the cakes and fry for 2 to 3 minutes, until crisp and golden brown. Turn and fry for 2 to 3 minutes, until crisp and brown, adding more oil if necessary. Transfer to paper towels to drain off any excess oil. Add the remaining 2 tablespoons oil to the sauté pan and fry the remaining 4 cakes. Drain on paper towels. Divide the cakes among 4 plates and keep warm.

In a large sauté pan, bring about 2 inches of water to a boil over high heat. Add the white vinegar and decrease the heat to achieve a simmer. Break 1 egg into a small dish and gently slide the egg into the water. Repeat for the remaining eggs. Cook for 3 to 4 minutes, until the whites are firm but the yolks are still runny. With a slotted spoon, remove and drain on a clean kitchen towel. Place an egg on top of each of the cakes. Spoon the sauce over the eggs and serve immediately.

Chuck's Lamb Chops Pupu

SERVES 6 TO 8

2 (1½- to 2-pound) racks of lamb

½ cup soy sauce

2 tablespoons hoisin sauce

2 tablespoons honey

2 teaspoons fresh grated ginger

1 tablespoon bottled chile pepper water (see page 26)

¼ cup beer

Pupu *is the Hawaiian word for hors d'oeurve. Master sommelier Chuck Furuya, a frequent guest on* Hawaii Cooks with Roy Yamaguchi, *often prepares succulent, tender lamb chops for casual pupu parties. Because lamb is a full-bodied meat, it is well suited to a marinade of robust hoisin sauce. Marinate these ahead of time and cook them as guests enjoy their Pineapple Vodka and Bloody Marys. No need for knives and forks: these chops are finger food.*

Remove the excess fat and membrane from the racks and French the bones, cutting out the meat between the bones and scraping the bones clean with a knife, leaving the chops intact. Cut the rack into individual chops and place them in a shallow dish in 1 layer.

In a small bowl, whisk together the soy sauce, hoisin sauce, honey, ginger, chile pepper water, and beer. Pour the marinade over the chops, turning and coating each chop well. Marinate for 4 hours, covered, in the refrigerator.

Prepare a hot fire in a charcoal grill or preheat a gas grill to high. Place the chops on the grill rack and grill for about 2 minutes, or until the edges are crispy and brown. Turn and cook the chops for another 2 minutes for medium rare, or to desired doneness. Transfer to a platter and serve immediately.

Pineapple Vodka

MAKES ABOUT 1 QUART

1/2 fresh pineapple, cut into 1-inch chunks

1 (750-ml) bottle vodka

Mint, for garnish

Place the pineapple in a quart-size covered glass jar or pitcher. Pour the vodka over, cover, and refrigerate for 4 to 5 days, allowing the pineapple to steep with the vodka.

To serve, pour into a chilled martini glass. Garnish with mint and serve immediately. (Pictured on page 81 with the Warm Tofu Salad.)

Bloody Mary

SERVES 1

Fresh lime wedge

Alaea (see page 15) or other coarse-grained salt

3/4 cup fresh tomato juice (page 155)

1 ounce vodka

1 teaspoon Worcestershire sauce

1/2 teaspoon bottled chile pepper water (see page 26)

Lemon grass stick, for garnish

Cilantro sprig, for garnish

Wet the rim of a tumbler with the lime then dip the rim into the salt.

Fill the tumbler with ice. Pour the tomato juice over the ice. Add the vodka, Worcestershire, and chile pepper water. Stir with the lemon grass stick and garnish with cilantro. Serve immediately.

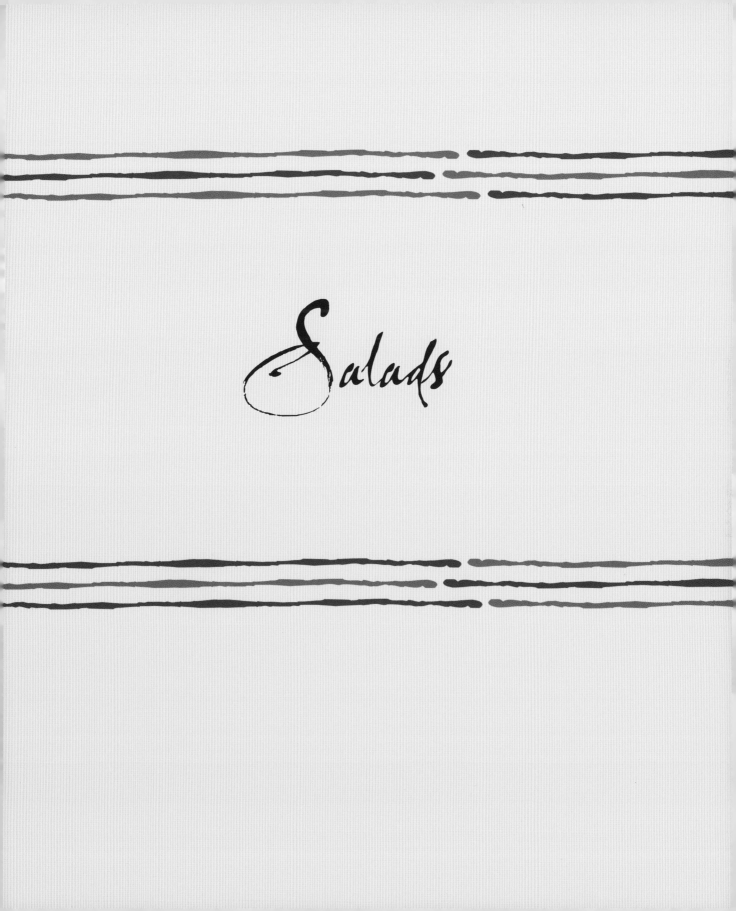

Salads

Roasted Duck Salad with Deep-Fried Tofu and Mango

SERVES 4

SALAD DRESSING

1/3 cup soy sauce

1 tablespoon sugar

3 tablespoons yuzu juice (see page 22) or freshly squeezed lemon or lime juice

1 tablespoon sesame oil

1 tablespoon sautéed garlic (page 151)

1 tablespoon sautéed ginger (page 151)

1 tablespoon sambal oelek or garlic chile paste (see page 26)

1 tablespoon freshly squeezed lemon juice

1 whole duck

Salt and freshly ground black pepper

2 tablespoons canola oil

SALAD

4 cups chicory

1 cup haricots verts

1 tablespoon canola oil, plus 3 cups for deep-frying

16 fresh shiitake mushrooms

10 ounces firm tofu

1 whole mango, firm but ripe, cut into bite-sized chunks

I like duck because it is succulent and fatty with gutsy flavor. I prefer the leg portions well done and caramelized over time, and the breast medium rare with a very crisp skin. It takes two cooking methods to do this but the results are well worth the effort. In this dish, hearty flavors combine with light ones and you'll experience a range of textures that will make eating a delight.

To prepare the dressing, in a bowl, whisk together the soy sauce, sugar, *yuzu* juice, sesame oil, sautéed garlic, sautéed ginger, *sambal oelek,* and lemon juice. Taste and adjust seasoning if necessary. Set aside.

Preheat the oven to 350°F.

To cut the duck into 4 pieces, cut along one side of the breastbone, easing the meat away from the bone to free one breast. Repeat for the other breast. Cut the joint where the thighs meet the breasts and remove the leg portion, leaving the thighbone intact to prevent shrinkage. Trim any excess fat from all the pieces.

Place an ovenproof sauté pan over medium-high heat. Season the legs with salt and pepper. Add 1 tablespoon of the oil to the pan. When the oil is hot, add the legs, meat side down. Sear for about 5 minutes, or until nicely browned, then turn so the skin side is down. Remove the pan from the heat and transfer to the oven. Roast for about 45 minutes, or until the legs are well browned, crisp, and cooked through.

In another sauté pan, heat the remaining 1 tablespoon oil over medium heat. Season the breasts with salt and pepper. Place the breasts in the pan skin side down. Cook for about 5 minutes, or until the skin is well browned and crisp. Turn and sear the other side for 2 to 3 minutes, until lightly browned. Remove from the pan and keep warm.

To prepare the salad, trim off and discard the green parts of the chicory, leaving the stems and white parts, which are firmer and slightly less bitter.

Bring a pot of water to a boil over high heat. Add a little salt and the *haricots verts.* Blanch for about 3 minutes, leaving the beans slightly crisp. Drain in a colander and immediately plunge into a bowl of ice water to stop the cooking. Drain again and pat dry.

Place a small sauté pan over high heat and add the 1 tablespoon oil. When the oil is hot, add the mushrooms and sauté for about 1 minute, or until the caps are browned. Season with salt and pepper.

Cut the tofu into 3/4-inch sticks. Drain on paper towels to remove any excess moisture. Heat a sauté pan over high heat and pour in the 3 cups oil. When the oil is hot (350°F), add the tofu pieces, a few at a time. Fry for 2 to 3 minutes, until golden brown and crisp. Remove from the oil and drain on paper towels.

To serve, divide the chicory among 4 individual plates. Arrange the *haricots verts,* mushrooms, tofu, and mango chunks on the chicory. Ladle half of the dressing over all. Slice each duck breast into 3 to 4 pieces and divide between 2 plates. Place the duck legs on the other 2 plates. Drizzle with the remaining dressing and serve.

Roy's Tips

Always use fresh oil for frying tofu. The first batch of tofu will brown quickly but as the tofu releases water and the oil becomes cloudy, it will take a little longer to fry and brown the pieces.

For another duck preparation, cook the duck as directed above and serve with the Honey Sauce (page 106).

Warm Tofu Salad of Wilted Greens and Macadamia Nuts

SERVES 4

20 ounces firm tofu

1/2 teaspoon salt

1/2 teaspoon shichimi (see page 28)

2 tablespoons macadamia nut oil

1 tablespoon sesame oil

2 teaspoons minced fresh garlic

2 teaspoons minced fresh ginger

1 ounce fresh shiitake mushrooms, sliced, about 1/2 cup

1 cup chopped mustard greens

1/2 cup sugar snap peas

1/2 cup bean sprouts

1/2 cup spinach leaves

1/2 cup radicchio

1 cup watercress, leaves and stems

3/4 ounce mung bean noodles, about 1/2 cup dry, soaked in water (see page 47)

2 tablespoons moromiso (see page 14)

2 tablespoons fish sauce

2 cups mesclun, for garnish

1/4 cup chopped macadamia nuts, for garnish

I love to eat tofu and I want everyone else to love it too. When fried, it has a little bit of chewiness and texture and pairs well with just about every sauce I can make. For a light but protein-rich entrée salad, try this one with crunchy greens and nuts.

Cut the tofu into triangle-shaped pieces about 1/2 inch thick. Lay the pieces on paper towels and press gently with more paper towels to remove excess moisture. Season each piece with salt and *shichimi.*

Heat a nonstick sauté pan over high heat and add 1 1/2 tablespoons of the macadamia nut oil. Sear the tofu for 2 to 3 minutes on each side, until golden brown. Drain on paper towels and keep warm.

Place a wok over high heat and add the remaining 1/2 tablespoon macadamia nut oil and the sesame oil. Add the garlic and ginger and stir-fry for 20 to 30 seconds, until barely light golden brown. Add the mushrooms, mustard greens, snap peas, bean sprouts, spinach, radicchio, and watercress and stir-fry for 2 minutes, or until the vegetables begin to wilt. Add the noodles, *moromiso,* and fish sauce, mix well, and stir-fry for 1 minute to blend the seasonings. Remove from the heat.

To serve, divide the fried tofu among 4 plates. Top each with mesclun and stir-fried vegetables. Sprinkle with the macadamia nuts and serve immediately.

Ahi Salad with Miso Dressing

SERVES 6

DRESSING

1/4 cup white miso

1/4 cup peanut oil

1/4 cup vegetable oil

2 tablespoons rice vinegar

1 tablespoon soy sauce

1 tablespoon mirin (see page 19)

2 tablespoons sugar

2 teaspoons grated fresh ginger

2 teaspoons toasted and ground
  sesame seeds (page 153)

1 daikon, cut crosswise into
  1/4-inch slices

1 pound won bok (napa cabbage),
  leaves separated

1/2 pound warabi (see page 44)

1 pound spinach, about 2 cups
  leaves, packed

2 tablespoons vegetable oil

1 long eggplant, cut diagonally into
  1/4-inch slices

6 (3-ounce) ahi fillets

Salt and freshly cracked black pepper

3 tablespoons chopped green onion,
  for garnish

2 tablespoons toasted sesame seeds,
  for garnish (page 153)

Big Island chef and caterer Faith Ogawa, a guest on the television show, created this hearty salad featuring fresh ahi from Island waters. Since ahi has a beef-like flavor and texture, it can take on the robust miso-based dressing and some unique, crunchy, Island-grown vegetables.

To prepare the dressing, combine all the ingredients in a small bowl and mix well with a whisk. Set aside.

In a large saucepan, bring water to a boil over high heat. Drop in the daikon slices and blanch for 1 minute to remove the sharp flavor. Remove with a slotted spoon and immediately plunge into a bowl of ice water to stop the cooking. Drain well and set aside.

In the same pan, blanch the won bok, *warabi,* and spinach in the same way, immersing each in boiling water for 1 to 2 minutes, until barely wilted but still crisp. Transfer to a bowl of ice water to stop the cooking. Drain each one well. Cut the won bok, *warabi,* and spinach into 2-inch pieces.

Place a sauté pan over high heat and add the oil. When the oil is hot, add the eggplant and fry for 30 to 45 seconds on each side, until golden brown and soft. Transfer to paper towels to remove any excess oil.

Season the ahi with salt and pepper. In the same sauté pan over high heat, sear the ahi pieces for 30 to 45 seconds per side, until lightly browned on both sides, adding more oil if necessary. Sear it longer if you prefer it cooked all the way through.

Divide the vegetables among 6 plates. Place the fish on top and garnish with the green onion and sesame seeds. Pour the dressing over and serve immediately.

Cured Salmon and Tomato Salad

SERVES 4

$^1/_2$ pound salmon fillet

Salt and freshly ground black pepper

5 tablespoons chopped fresh tarragon

Juice of 2 limes

$^1/_2$ cup extra virgin olive oil

4 large red tomatoes, sliced

4 large zebra or other sweet tomatoes, sliced

1 pound fresh whole-milk mozzarella cheese, sliced

2 cups arugula

12 sweet basil leaves, torn

4 sprigs tarragon, for garnish

$^1/_2$ cup shaved Parmesan cheese, for garnish

In this recipe, the acidity of lime juice "cooks" the salmon and also becomes the base for the salad dressing. Extra virgin olive oil balances the tartness while ripe tomatoes, spicy arugula, and herbs punctuate the creaminess of mozzarella. This is a simple and delicious salad, perfect for Hawaii's tropical climate especially because there's no cooking involved.

Cut the salmon fillets into $^1/_4$-inch-thick slices and place on a large plate in a single layer. Season the salmon with salt, pepper, and 2 tablespoons of the tarragon. Pour the lime juice over the salmon, then pour $^1/_4$ cup of the oil over. Marinate for 15 to 20 minutes, until the surface of the salmon becomes opaque.

Divide the red tomatoes, zebra tomatoes, and mozzarella among 4 plates and season with salt and pepper. Drizzle with 3 tablespoons of the oil.

In a bowl, combine the arugula and basil leaves. Drizzle with the remaining 1 tablespoon oil and gently toss to coat the greens. Season with salt and pepper.

Place the salmon on top of the tomatoes and sprinkle with the remaining 3 tablespoons tarragon. Pile the arugula on top of the salmon. Garnish with a sprig of tarragon and the Parmesan cheese. Serve immediately.

Roy's Tips

Use the best extra virgin olive oil you have in your pantry. I prefer those that are fruity and light without the grassy note that some can have.

Accompany this salad with crusty bread to sop up the dressing.

Seared Scallop Salad with Mangoes and Fruit Vinaigrette

SERVES 4

VINAIGRETTE

3/4 cup puréed fresh strawberries

1/4 cup sugar

1 teaspoon chopped fresh mint

1 teaspoon minced lemon grass

2 tablespoons chopped shallots

2 tablespoons freshly squeezed
   lemon juice

1/4 cup passion fruit vinegar
   (see page 23)

Salt and freshly ground black pepper

3 artichokes

1 cup green beans

1 tablespoon olive oil

2 teaspoons minced lemon grass

2 teaspoons minced fresh garlic

16 scallops

3 cups chopped chicory, green tops
   trimmed

1 cup sliced fresh mango

1/4 cup kaiware, for garnish
   (see page 41)

The citrusy note of lemon grass on tender, soft, delicate scallops is picked up in a lively fruit vinaigrette that stands up to bitter chicory and distinctive artichokes. Mango adds its creaminess without being rich in this refreshing and substantial salad.

To prepare the vinaigrette, in a blender, combine the strawberry purée, sugar, mint, lemon grass, shallots, lemon juice, and vinegar. Blend to a smooth consistency. Season with salt and pepper to taste. Set aside.

In the bottom of a steamer, bring water to a boil over high heat. Decrease the heat to achieve a simmer. Place the artichokes in the steamer basket and position over the water. Cover and steam for 25 to 35 minutes, until a fork easily pierces the bottom of the heart at the stem. Remove the artichokes and allow to cool. Break off the leaves to expose the fuzzy choke. With a spoon, scrape away the choke, leaving the heart. Cut off the stem and slice the artichoke heart into 1/4-inch pieces. Set aside.

Bring a pot of water to a boil over high heat. Add a little salt and the green beans. Blanch for about 3 minutes, leaving the beans slightly crisp. Drain in a colander and immediately plunge into a bowl of ice water to stop the cooking. Drain again and pat dry.

In a bowl, combine the olive oil, lemon grass, and garlic. Add the scallops and mix well. Season with salt and pepper. Place a sauté pan over high heat. Add the scallops and sear, turning once, for 1 minute on each side, or until browned on the edges. Transfer to a plate and keep warm.

Combine the artichoke hearts, green beans, and chicory in a bowl and mix with 6 tablespoons of the vinaigrette.

Divide the salad among 4 plates and top with the mango and *kaiware*. Arrange the scallops around the salad. Drizzle the plate with the remaining vinaigrette or serve it alongside.

Roy's Tip

You can substitute another fruit-flavored vinegar for the passion fruit vinegar.

Pickled Mango Vinaigrette

MAKES 2¹/₂ CUPS

2 egg yolks

5 teaspoons red wine vinegar

1 cup pickled mango juice

1¹/₂ cups vegetable oil

1 teaspoon dry mustard, mixed with enough water to form a paste

1¹/₂ teaspoons freshly crushed black peppercorns

2 teaspoons freshly squeezed lime juice

3 tablespoons pickled mango, cut into ¹/₄-inch dice

Pinch of salt

Years ago, when a student brought some pickled mangoes to chef Alan Wong, a light went on, sparking the creativity of one of Hawaii's foremost chefs. Known for his whimsical takeoff on Island foods at his popular Alan Wong's Restaurant, this recipe, demonstrated on the TV show, epitomizes Chef Wong's playful but serious intentions.

Pickled mango is a popular island treat made of green mangoes, vinegar, salt, and sugar. It is found at roadside stands, small markets, and home kitchens during the summer mango season. The pickling liquid is tart and provides the acidic base for this vinaigrette.

Combine all the ingredients in a blender and blend for 2 to 3 minutes, until well mixed and smooth. Use as a dressing for salad greens. The dressing can be stored in a covered jar in the refrigerator for a week.

Roy's Tip

Chef Wong likes to serve this vinaigrette with a simple mesclun salad and an equally simple Pan-Seared Chicken (page 106).

Entrées

Grilled Chuck Steak with Pad Thai-Style Noodles

SERVES 4

2 pounds (1¹/₂-inch-thick) chuck steak

Garlic powder

Hawaiian salt or other coarse-grained salt

Freshly cracked black pepper

¹/₂ pound Iwamoto saimin noodles (see page 48)

7 tablespoons vegetable oil

1 cup broccolini, cut into bite-sized pieces

2 teaspoons minced fresh garlic

2 teaspoons minced fresh ginger

2 ounces fresh shiitake mushrooms, julienned, about 1 cup

1 cup snow peas, strings removed

1 cup julienned bamboo shoots

1 cup baby corn

3 tablespoons oyster sauce

2 teaspoons sugar

3 tablespoons sake

2 teaspoons cornstarch

1 tablespoon sesame oil

¹/₂ cup julienned yellow bell pepper, for garnish

¹/₂ cup julienned red bell pepper, for garnish

1 cup bean sprouts, for garnish

¹/₂ cup corn sprouts, for garnish

¹/₂ cup chopped macadamia nuts, for garnish

2 red jalapeño chiles, sliced thin, for garnish

There's nothing like a simple grilled steak, especially a thick chuck steak, a cut with great flavor. A basic seasoning rub is all you need to make this inexpensive cut of meat taste superb. I use garlic powder in this instance because fresh garlic would burn and become bitter as you grill the steak. Paired with a crispy noodle cake topped with lots of crunchy vegetables and nuts just like traditional pad Thai, this is a wonderful meal.

Season the steak generously with the garlic powder, salt, and pepper. Rub the seasonings into the steak. Cover and refrigerate for 30 minutes.

To prepare the noodles, bring a large pot of water to a boil over high heat. Add the noodles, bring the water back to a boil and cook for 1 minute, or until tender. Transfer to a colander and drain.

Heat a nonstick sauté pan over medium heat and add 2 tablespoons of the oil. Add the noodles to the pan and spread them to form a cake-like layer. Fry for 6 to 8 minutes, pressing the noodles into a cake, until golden brown and crisp. Turn over, add 1 tablespoon of the oil, and brown the other side for 6 to 8 minutes. Transfer to a platter and keep warm.

Prepare a hot fire in a charcoal grill or preheat a gas grill to medium-high. Pour 2 tablespoons of the oil over the steak. Place the steak on the grill rack and grill, turning once, for 7 to 8 minutes on each side for medium rare, or to desired doneness. Remove from the grill and let stand for 10 to 15 minutes.

Place a wok over medium-high heat. Add the remaining 2 tablespoons oil and when it is hot, add the broccolini and cook for 2 minutes, tossing with a spatula, until half cooked. Make a well in the center of the wok and add the garlic and ginger, adding more oil if necessary. Stir-fry for 20 to 30 seconds, until barely light golden brown and mix with the broccolini. Add the mushrooms, snow peas, bamboo shoots, and baby corn and stir-fry for 2 to 3 minutes, until the snow peas are half cooked. Stir in the oyster sauce, sugar, and 2 tablespoons of the sake and mix well. Mix the remaining 1 tablespoon sake with the cornstarch and add to the wok. Toss for 1 minute to mix, drizzle the sesame oil over, mix again, and turn off the heat.

To serve, arrange the stir-fried vegetables on top of the noodles. Garnish with the yellow bell pepper, red bell pepper, bean sprouts, corn sprouts, nuts, and jalapeños. Slice the steak into $1/2$-inch-thick pieces and arrange it on a separate serving platter. Serve immediately.

Roy's Tips

In place of the Iwamoto saimin *noodles you can substitute* yaki soba, *ramen, chow mein, or another* saimin *noodle.*

To remove the canned flavor from bamboo shoots and baby corn, drain and rinse well under tap water. A brief immersion into boiling water will also help to refresh their flavor.

Asian-Style Spicy Peppercorn Steak

SERVES 4

VEGETABLES

8 thick onion rings

1/2 cup flour

1 egg, beaten

3/4 cup panko (see page 48)

2 cups canola oil

1 tablespoon olive oil

8 ounces spinach leaves, about
  2 cups

2 teaspoons minced fresh garlic

Salt

4 ounces button mushrooms, sliced,
  about 1 cup

4 (8-ounce) New York strip steaks

1/2 cup plus 1 teaspoon freshly
  cracked black peppercorns

1 teaspoon shichimi (see page 28)

4 teaspoons chopped lemon grass

1 tablespoon canola oil

2 tablespoons unsalted butter

2 shallots, minced

1 teaspoon minced fresh garlic

1/4 cup cognac

3/4 cup heavy cream

1 teaspoon soy sauce

2 cups cooked short-grain white rice,
  for serving

Green onions, cut into 4-inch lengths,
  for garnish

A thick, succulent beef steak can stand up to the strongest of seasonings, which is why peppercorn-crusted steak is a classic. In my version, the heat of black peppercorns is boosted by shichimi, *the Japanese seven-spice mixture; lemon grass adds a refreshing and exotic Asian note. The rich, creamy pungent sauce will make this steak outstanding.*

Coat the onion rings with the flour, dip in the egg, and coat with *panko.* Heat the canola oil in a sauté pan over medium-high heat. When the oil is hot (350°F), add the onion rings and fry for 2 to 3 minutes, until golden brown. Lift from the oil and drain on paper towels. Keep warm.

Heat a sauté pan over high heat and add 1/2 tablespoon of the olive oil. Add the spinach and 1 teaspoon of the garlic, sprinkle with a pinch of salt, and sauté for 15 seconds, or until wilted. Transfer to a plate and keep warm.

In the same sauté pan, add the remaining 1/2 tablespoon olive oil. Add the mushrooms and the remaining 1 teaspoon garlic and sauté for 1 minute, or until cooked through and lightly browned. Season with salt and mix well. Transfer to a plate and keep warm.

To prepare the steaks, sprinkle both sides with the 1/2 cup peppercorns, *shichimi,* and lemon grass. Season with salt.

Heat a heavy sauté pan over medium-high heat. When the pan is hot, add the oil and the steaks. Cook, turning once, for about 2 minutes on each side for rare, or to desired doneness. Transfer the steaks to a plate and keep warm.

In the same sauté pan over medium-high heat, add 1 tablespoon of the butter, shallots, garlic, and the 1 teaspoon peppercorns. Sauté for 30 to 45 seconds, until the shallots and garlic are lightly browned. Pour in the cognac, light a match to it, and burn off the alcohol. When the flame subsides, add the cream and mix well. Decrease the heat to medium-low and simmer for 3 to 5 minutes, until reduced by one-third. Add the soy sauce and stir. Taste the sauce and adjust with salt if necessary. Add the remaining 1 tablespoon butter and whisk in.

To serve, divide the rice among 4 plates. Divide the spinach and mushrooms over the rice and top with a steak. Spoon the sauce to one side of the plate. Garnish with the onion rings and arrange the green onions in a crisscross pattern.

Portuguese-Style Steak Sandwich with Spicy Soy Dipping Sauce

SERVES 4

SAUCE

3/4 cup reduced-sodium soy sauce

1/2 cup Lingham chile sauce or other sweet chile sauce

1/4 cup sugar

1 tablespoon sautéed garlic (page 151)

1 tablespoon sautéed ginger (page 151)

1 tablespoon minced green onion

STEAK

1/4 cup red wine vinegar

4 cloves fresh garlic, minced

1/4 cup unsalted butter, melted

1 1/2 pounds sirloin steak

1/4 cup unsalted butter, at room temperature

1 Maui or other sweet onion, sliced

2 cloves fresh garlic, minced

2 tomatoes, diced

1 tablespoon white balsamic vinegar

1 tablespoon chopped fresh parsley

Salt and freshly ground black pepper

4 taro rolls, halved

1 clove fresh garlic, minced

2 tablespoons unsalted butter, at room temperature

Portuguese immigrants from the Azores settled in Hawaii in the late nineteenth century, adding to the cultural mix of the Islands. Their foods are an important part of the Islands' cuisine, especially vinha d'alhos, *a vinegar, garlic, and chile pepper marinade used with pork, turkey, and other meats. Here, the vinegar and garlic are infused into a steak and the heat is in the dipping sauce of this open-faced sandwich.*

To prepare the sauce, combine all the ingredients in a bowl and mix well.

To prepare the steak, combine the vinegar, garlic, and melted butter in a flat dish. Place the steak in the marinade, turning and coating well. Cover and refrigerate for 30 minutes.

Heat a sauté pan over medium-high heat. Add the room temperature butter and when it is sizzling, add the onion and garlic and sauté for 2 to 3 minutes, until soft. Add the tomatoes, vinegar, and parsley and cook for 2 minutes, or until the tomatoes are cooked through. Season with salt and pepper. Remove from the heat and set aside.

Prepare a hot fire in a charcoal grill or preheat a gas grill to medium-high. Remove the steak from the marinade and season with salt and pepper. Place the steak on the grill and cook, turning once, for 3 to 4 minutes on each side for rare, or to desired doneness. Transfer to a cutting board and let stand for 5 minutes.

Heat a broiler and position a rack 4 inches from the heating element. Place the rolls on a baking sheet, cut side up. Blend the garlic with the butter and spread the mixture on the rolls. Place under the broiler for 1 to 2 minutes, until golden brown, watching so that the rolls do not burn.

To serve, place 2 roll halves side by side on each of 4 plates. Slice the steak and arrange on top of the rolls. Top the steak with the onion mixture. Serve immediately with the sauce on the side.

Roy's Tip

Taro rolls are a Hawaiian specialty, a soft, purplish-gray dinner roll that includes poi as an ingredient. Any soft dinner roll or a hamburger bun can be substituted.

Lamb Steaks with Okinawan Sweet Potato Mash and Apple-Curry Sauce

SERVES 4

SAUCE

2 tablespoons macadamia nut oil

1 cup diced sweet apple, about
  1 whole apple

1/2 cup chopped carrot

1/2 cup chopped celery

1/2 cup chopped onion

2 tablespoons sliced fresh ginger

6 cloves garlic

1/2 cup cilantro, leaves and stems

1/4 cup minced lemon grass

1 tablespoon coriander seeds

3 tablespoons yellow curry powder

2 cups veal or chicken stock
  (pages 156 and 150)

SWEET POTATO MASH

4 Okinawan sweet potatoes
  (see page 48)

1/2 cup heavy cream

1/4 cup unsalted butter

Salt and freshly ground black pepper

4 (6-ounce) lamb leg steaks

1 tablespoon minced fresh garlic

1 tablespoon Hawaiian salt or other
  coarse-grained salt

2 tablespoons canola oil

1/4 cup chopped macadamia nuts,
  for garnish

Parsley leaves, for garnish

Robust, chewy lamb is paired with a spicy Indian-style curry sauce that takes on a sweet note from apples. Sugary and purple-hued sweet potatoes balance the spicy, ochre-colored curry, a striking presenation.

To prepare the sauce, heat a sauté pan over medium-high heat and add the oil. When the oil is hot, add the apple, carrot, celery, onion, ginger, garlic, cilantro, lemon grass, and coriander seeds. Sauté for about 3 minutes, or until all the ingredients are golden brown. Add the curry powder and stock and bring to a boil. Decrease the heat to low and simmer, uncovered, for 30 minutes, or until reduced by half. Taste and adjust seasoning, adding salt and sugar if necessary. Strain the sauce and keep warm.

To prepare the mash, place the sweet potatoes in a saucepan with 2 cups of water. Place over high heat, cover, and bring to a boil. Decrease the heat to achieve a simmer and cook for 20 to 30 minutes, until fork-tender. Remove from the heat, drain, and when cool enough to handle, peel. Place in a bowl and mash with a potato masher. Add the cream and butter and mix well. Season with salt and pepper. Keep warm.

Season the steaks with garlic and salt. Heat a heavy sauté pan over high heat and add the oil. When the oil is hot, add the steaks and sear, turning once, for 1 to 2 minutes on each side for medium rare, or to desired doneness. Remove the steaks from the pan and allow to rest for 5 minutes. Cut into 1/2-inch slices.

To serve, divide the sweet potatoes among 4 plates. Place the sliced lamb on top and spoon the curry sauce around. Sprinkle with macadamia nuts and garnish with parsley leaves.

Roy's Tip

For this recipe, use a sweet apple like Fuji, Gala, or Golden Delicious.

Mediterranean-Style Lamb with Crispy Ginger

SERVES 4

DRESSING

¹/₄ cup olive oil

2 tablespoons minced fresh garlic

2 tablespoons minced fresh ginger

2 tablespoons minced shallot

2 teaspoons fresh chopped thyme

2 teaspoons fresh minced sweet basil

2 tablespoons soy sauce

2 tablespoons freshly squeezed lemon juice

6 tablespoons olive oil

8 (³/₈-inch-thick) slices small globe eggplant, quartered

Salt and freshly ground black pepper

2 small tomatoes, cut into chunks

1 tablespoon minced fresh garlic

3 tablespoons chopped fresh sweet basil

8 (3-ounce) lamb loin chops

4 teaspoons fresh thyme leaves

1 cup canola oil

¹/₄ cup julienned fresh ginger, for garnish

2 cups mesclun, for garnish

When I think of Mediterranean flavors, tomatoes, eggplant, garlic, herbs, olive oil, and lamb come to mind, all of which are presented in this meal. Crispy ginger is the surprise here, an assertive flavor accent for the lamb that is echoed in the vinaigrette. And of course, there's a little soy sauce, the essential salt element.

To prepare the dressing, heat the oil in a sauté pan over medium-high heat. When the oil is hot, add the garlic, ginger, shallot, thyme, and basil and sauté for 1 minute, or until lightly browned. Add the soy sauce and lemon juice and stir. Remove from the heat and cool.

Heat 3 tablespoons of the olive oil in a sauté pan over high heat. Add the eggplant and cook for 2 to 3 minutes, until browned. Transfer to a plate and season with salt and pepper. Keep warm.

In the same pan, heat 1 tablespoon of the olive oil. Add the tomato, garlic, and basil and sauté for 1 to 2 minutes, to cook the garlic and blend the flavors. Transfer the tomato mixture to a plate and season with salt and pepper. Keep warm.

Season the lamb with the thyme, salt, and pepper. Coat the lamb with the remaining 2 tablespoons olive oil. In the same sauté pan over high heat, sear the lamb, turning once, for 1 to 2 minutes on each side for rare, or to desired doneness. Transfer to a plate and allow to rest for 5 minutes.

To prepare the ginger, heat the canola oil in a small sauté pan over medium-high heat. Drop in the ginger and deep-fry for 2 to 3 minutes, until brown and crisp. Drain on paper towels.

To serve, divide the eggplant among 4 plates. Top with the greens and the tomatoes. Arrange the lamb on top of the vegetables. Drizzle the vinaigrette over the lamb and garnish with the ginger.

Roast Pork with Caramelized Pineapple

SERVES 4

2 pounds boneless pork shoulder or butt, trimmed of fat

PINEAPPLE MARINADE

1 cup canned pineapple juice

3 bay leaves

$1/2$ cup sliced celery

$1/4$ onion, sliced

4 ($1/4$-inch) slices fresh ginger

1 tablespoon whole black peppercorns

1 tablespoon whole cloves

3 star anise

1 tablespoon chopped cilantro

2 green onions, coarsely chopped

3 slices of rind from a fresh pineapple

HONEY GLAZE

1 cup honey

1 tablespoon minced fresh garlic

1 tablespoon minced fresh ginger

2 teaspoons sautéed garlic (page 151)

2 teaspoons sautéed ginger (page 151)

2 teaspoons sautéed shallots (page 153)

2 tablespoons white balsamic vinegar

5 tablespoons extra virgin olive oil

4 caramelized pineapple slices, chopped, plus additional for garnish (page 152)

2 cups mesclun

Fresh, ripe, juicy pineapple is a wonderful match with fatty pork. In this dish, the acidity of pineapple juice helps to tenderize the pork as it marinates; a honey glaze caramelizes as the pork roasts; and slices of golden brown pineapple accentuate the fruity note. The pork needs to marinate overnight so plan ahead.

To prepare the pork, tie it with kitchen string to form a compact roast. Combine all the marinade ingredients in a large bowl. Place the pork in the marinade, coating it well. Cover and marinate overnight in the refrigerator, turning once or twice.

Preheat the oven to 350°F.

Combine the honey glaze ingredients in a small bowl and mix well.

Remove the pork from the marinade and place in a roasting pan. Discard the marinade. Coat the pork with the honey glaze. Place the pan in the oven and cook for 50 to 60 minutes, until the pork is cooked through and an instant-read thermometer registers 140°F. Remove from the oven and keep warm.

Combine the sautéed garlic, sautéed ginger, sautéed shallots, vinegar, oil, and pineapple in a bowl and mix well with a whisk.

To serve, slice the pork into $1/2$-inch-thick slices and arrange 3 or 4 slices on each of 4 plates. Place the greens next to the pork and drizzle the garlic-ginger dressing over both. Garnish with caramelized pineapple and serve at once.

Kalua Pork with Taro Sauce and Tofu-Yuba Stir-Fry

SERVES 6

2 pounds boneless pork shoulder
  or butt

3 cups chicken stock (page 150)

MISO GLAZE

$1/2$ cup white miso

1 cup mirin (see page 19)

3 tablespoons sugar

$1/2$ cup cooked taro or spinach leaves,
  coarsely chopped (page 156)

$1/2$ cup veal demi-glace (page 156)

$1/2$ cup coconut milk

2 tablespoons minced fresh ginger

Salt

STIR-FRY

2 tablespoons teriyaki sauce
  (page 154)

1 tablespoon white miso

2 tablespoons vegetable oil

1 bitter melon, halved, cored, and cut
  into $1/2$-inch-thick slices

1 tablespoon minced fresh garlic

1 tablespoon minced fresh ginger

$1/2$ cup julienned red bell pepper

$1/2$ cup julienned yellow bell pepper

1 yuba sheet (see page 46)

10 ounces firm tofu, drained and cut
  into 4 by $3/4$-inch pieces

Kalua pork is a Hawaiian favorite: tender, smoky, and a little salty, often made with fatty pork butt or shoulder. I like a miso glaze with the smoky pork and a rich, creamy taro sauce, a variation on traditional Hawaiian luau dishes. But I've also included a stir-fry that combines four soy products and bitter melon, all robustly seasoned. Since the tofu and yuba stir-fry is protein rich, it could serve as a vegetarian entrée.

Cut the pork into 2-inch-thick slabs and place in a shallow heatproof pan. Pour the chicken stock over the pork.

Soak 2 cups of wood smoking chips in a bowl of water for 10 minutes. Remove the grill rack from a charcoal or gas grill. Prepare a hot fire in the charcoal grill or preheat the gas grill to medium; when the charcoal is white hot, allow it to cool to medium. Push the coals to opposite sides of the grill. Drain the chips, place them in a heatproof pan, and position in the middle of the coals. Replace the grill rack.

Place the pan with the pork on the grill rack and cover the grill. Smoke for 1 to $1^{1/2}$ hours, until the pork takes on a smoky flavor but is still not quite tender.

Transfer the pork and its liquid to a large saucepan. Place the pan over high heat and bring to a boil. Decrease the heat to low and cook for 1 to $1^{1/2}$ hours, covered, until the pork is fork-tender. Reserve 1 cup of the braising liquid.

To prepare the glaze, combine the miso, mirin, and sugar in a small saucepan over medium heat. Bring to a boil, then decrease the heat to achieve a simmer. Cook for 10 to 15 minutes, until the glaze is very thick and reduced by half.

To prepare the sauce, combine the taro, demi-glace, and reserved braising liquid in a saucepan over medium-high heat. Cook for 5 to 10 minutes, until reduced by half. Add the coconut milk and mix well. Place the ginger in your hand and squeeze, extracting the juice into the taro mixture; discard the ginger. Mix well and continue to cook for another 3 minutes, or until warmed through. Taste and adjust the seasoning with salt if necessary. Keep warm.

To prepare the stir-fry, place a wok over high heat. In a small bowl, whisk together the teriyaki sauce and miso. Add the oil to the wok and when it is hot, add the bitter melon and stir-fry for 2 minutes, until lightly brown and tender. Add the garlic and ginger and mix well. Add the red bell pepper, yellow bell pepper, and *yuba* and stir-fry for 2 minutes, until lightly browned. Add the tofu and mix gently. Drizzle the teriyaki sauce over the mixture and mix well. Continue to cook for 1 minute, or until the tofu is warmed through. Remove the wok from the heat and transfer the vegetables to a serving platter.

To serve, cut the pork into thick slices and place on top of the vegetables. Drizzle the pork with the glaze. Ladle the sauce around the platter. Serve immediately.

Roy's Tips

You can oven-smoke and braise the pork by placing it in a shallow pan with the stock. Add 1 to 2 teaspoons of liquid smoke. Place the pan in a 325°F oven for 2¹/₂ to 3 hours, until fork-tender.

The miso glaze will provide plenty of salty flavor; don't be tempted to salt the pork.

Foo jook, dried Chinese tofu skins, can be substituted for yuba. Use 2 "sticks" or 1 sheet of foo jook, reconstituted in water and sliced.

To remove some of the bitterness, you can slice and blanch bitter melon for 1 minute before stir-frying.

Char Siu Pork Chops with Black Bean Sauce and Stir-Fried Vegetables

SERVES 4

SAUCE

2 tablespoons fermented black beans (see page 13)

2 tablespoons sesame oil

1 tablespoon minced fresh garlic

1 tablespoon minced fresh ginger

1 tablespoon minced green onion

1/3 cup red wine

1/2 cup bottled clam juice

1/2 cup veal demi-glace (page 156)

2 teaspoons sugar

2 teaspoons oyster sauce

2 tablespoons unsalted butter

PORK CHOPS

1/2 cup bottled char siu sauce

2 tablespoons hoisin sauce

4 (1 1/2-inch-thick) pork chops, trimmed of fat

2 tablespoons vegetable oil

STIR-FRIED VEGETABLES

2 tablespoons sesame oil

1/2 teaspoon minced fresh garlic

1/2 teaspoon minced fresh ginger

1/2 cup julienned red bell pepper

1/2 cup julienned yellow bell pepper

1 cup (1-inch) pieces yard-long beans or green beans

Julienned green onion, for garnish

This contemporary preparation combines classic Chinese flavors with the rich traditions of French cuisine. The sharpness of fermented black beans in the sauce mellows with the addition of veal stock and butter. I call this a good fortune pork chop because char siu *sauce adds the color red, a symbol of good luck for the lunar New Year.*

To prepare the sauce, in a small bowl, soak the fermented black beans in water for 5 minutes. Drain and mince.

Place a saucepan over medium-high heat. Add 1 tablespoon of the oil with the garlic, ginger, and green onion and sauté for 20 to 30 seconds, until barely light golden brown. Add the remaining 1 tablespoon oil, then add the black beans and cook for 2 minutes, or until the seasonings are aromatic. Add the wine and bring to a boil for 2 to 3 minutes. Add the clam juice and bring to a boil for 2 to 3 minutes. Add the demi-glace and bring to a boil for 2 to 3 minutes. Whisk in the sugar and oyster sauce and blend well. Taste and adjust the seasoning with sugar if necessary. Add the butter and mix well. Decrease the heat to achieve a bare simmer and keep the sauce warm.

Preheat the oven to 325°F. Combine the *char siu* sauce and hoisin sauce in a bowl and mix well. Coat the pork chops with the marinade.

Heat a large ovenproof sauté pan over high heat. Add the oil and when the oil is hot, add the chops and sear for 3 to 4 minutes, until caramelized and brown. Turn and sear the other side for 3 to 4 minutes, until caramelized and brown (do not allow to blacken). Remove the pan from the heat and place in the oven to finish cooking the chops, about 10 minutes, or until an instant-read thermometer registers 140°F.

To prepare the vegetables, place a wok over high heat. Add the oil, garlic, and ginger and stir-fry for 20 to 30 seconds, until barely light golden brown. Add the red bell pepper, yellow bell pepper, and beans and cook for 3 to 4 minutes, until cooked but still crunchy.

To serve, spoon a pool of sauce onto each of 4 plates. Divide the vegetables among the plates and place a pork chop on top of each pile of vegetables. Garnish with the green onion and serve immediately.

Tuscan-Style Pasta with White Beans and Pork

SERVES 6 TO 8

2 pounds boneless pork butt
  or shoulder

Salt and freshly ground black pepper

9 tablespoons olive oil

2 tablespoons minced fresh garlic

3/4 cup minced pancetta

3/4 cup minced carrot

3/4 cup minced celery

3/4 cup minced onion

10 to 15 fresh sweet basil leaves

1 tablespoon minced fresh thyme,
  plus 2 tablespoons for garnish

1 cup dried white navy beans

8 cups veal or chicken stock
  (pages 156 and 150)

1 pound penne pasta

4 ounces button mushrooms,
  quartered, about 1 cup

8 ounces fresh spinach leaves, about
  1 cup firmly packed

1 cup basic tomato sauce (page 155)

Extra virgin olive oil, for garnish

Cracked black peppercorns,
  for garnish

2 tablespoons chopped fresh flat-leaf
  parsley, for garnish

I prepare this robust casserole for gatherings at home. Tender, chewy pork butt—a cut I love for its fattiness and near-sweetness when well cooked—and soft pasta and beans are richly flavored with a classic mirepoix (carrot, celery, onion), stock, and lots of fresh herbs. Pancetta provides the salt, and mushrooms add their earthy quality; all the flavors blend into a savory dish that needs little more than perhaps a fruity red wine.

Season the pork lightly with salt and pepper. Place a large saucepan over medium-high heat. Add 4 tablespoons of the olive oil to the saucepan. When the oil is hot, add the pork and sear for 8 to 10 minutes, until golden brown on all sides. Transfer to a plate.

In the same pan, add 1 tablespoon of the garlic and 1/2 cup of the pancetta. Cook for 1 to 2 minutes, until the garlic is light golden brown. Add the carrot, celery, onion, basil, and thyme and cook for 2 to 3 minutes, until the vegetables are browned. Return the pork to the pan. Add the beans and stock and bring to a boil. Decrease the heat to achieve a simmer and continue to cook, uncovered, for 1 1/2 to 2 hours, until the beans are soft, the pork is tender, and the stock is reduced by about half. Turn off the heat and skim any excess fat off the top. Transfer the pork to a cutting board and tent with aluminum foil to keep warm.

Place a large pot of water over high heat and bring to a boil. Add 1 table-spoon of salt to the water, then add the pasta and cook for 8 to 10 minutes, until tender. Drain in a colander and transfer to a bowl. Toss with 3 table-spoons of the olive oil and set aside.

Place a sauté pan over medium-high heat. Add the remaining 2 table-spoons olive oil, 1 tablespoon garlic, and 1/4 cup pancetta and cook for 2 to 3 minutes, until the garlic is light golden brown. Add the mushrooms and cook for 1 to 2 minutes, until they start to brown. Add the spinach and sauté for 30 seconds, until wilted. Transfer to the pot of beans.

Reheat the beans over medium-low heat. Add the tomato sauce and the pasta and mix well. Continue to cook for 5 to 10 minutes, until the flavors blend and the mixture is hot. Adjust seasoning with salt and pepper.

To serve, slice the pork into 1/2-inch-thick pieces. Mound a serving of pasta and beans in the center of each plate. Drizzle with olive oil and season with peppercorns. Place a serving of pork on top of the beans and garnish with thyme and parsley.

Salt-Crusted Cornish Game Hen with Thai Black Rice Risotto

SERVES 4

GAME HENS

4 Cornish game hens

5 pounds Hawaiian or kosher salt

$^1/_2$ cup minced fresh ginger

$^1/_2$ cup grated lemon zest

MANGO SAUCE

2 cups puréed ripe mango

$^1/_2$ teaspoon salt

1 tablespoon freshly squeezed lemon juice

1 tablespoon extra virgin olive oil

RISOTTO

1 cup Thai black rice (see page 49)

1 cup water

$^1/_2$ cup coconut milk

1 tablespoon vegetable oil

2 green onions, chopped, about $^1/_2$ cup

2 ounces diced char siu, about $^1/_2$ cup (see page 51)

2 ounces diced Portuguese sausage, about $^1/_2$ cup (see page 51)

2 teaspoons minced fresh ginger

1 to 2 Thai bird chiles, finely diced

2 tablespoons toasted coconut flakes (page 150)

$^3/_4$ cup diced firm, ripe mango

1 teaspoon salt

Salt is a crucial seasoning in cooking. But it can also be a cooking medium, transmitting heat and sealing in the juices of a Cornish game hen. I like to use coarse-grained Hawaiian salt for this preparation because it doesn't melt away. The hens will not turn brown but the purplish risotto and the mango sauce will provide plenty of color on the plate.

Preheat the oven to 450°F.

Rinse the Cornish game hens and pat dry. Tie the legs together with kitchen string.

Pour about $1^1/_2$ pounds of the salt in the bottom of a deep pot or casserole dish large enough to comfortably but snugly hold all the game hens. Place the hens on top of the salt.

Mix the remaining $3^1/_2$ pounds salt with the ginger and lemon zest and pour over the hens, completely covering them on the sides and top. Place the pot in the oven and bake for 1 hour.

Insert an instant-read thermometer through the salt crust and into a hen. The hen is done when the temperature reads 160°F. Remove the pot from the oven and let rest for 10 minutes.

While the game hens are baking, make the mango sauce. In a small saucepan, combine the puréed mango, salt, lemon juice, and olive oil and bring to a boil over high heat. Decrease the heat to medium-low and simmer for about 30 minutes, until the mangoes are reduced to a thick, pulpy mixture. Keep warm.

Meanwhile, to prepare the risotto, place the rice and water in a saucepan, cover, and bring to a boil over high heat. Decrease the heat to low and simmer for about 15 minutes. Add the coconut milk, stir, and continue to cook, covered, for another 15 minutes, until the rice is cooked through but not mushy, adding a little more water if necessary. It is important not to overcook the rice.

(continued)

SALT-CRUSTED CORNISH GAME HEN, *continued*

While the rice is cooking, heat a small sauté pan over high heat and add the oil. When the oil is hot, add the green onions, *char siu,* and sausage and sauté for 1 to 2 minutes, until lightly browned. Add the ginger, chiles, coconut, and diced mango and cook for 2 minutes, until the ginger is lightly browned.

When the rice is cooked, transfer the green onion-mango mixture to the saucepan with the rice, add the salt, and mix well. Taste and adjust seasoning, adding more salt if necessary. Keep warm.

With a spoon, break through the crust on the hens and carefully remove the salt. Gently lift each hen from the salt and brush off any excess.

Divide the risotto among 4 plates and place a hen on top of the risotto. Spoon the mango sauce over the hens and around the plates. Serve immediately.

Roy's Tip

You could substitute a whole 3- to 4-pound broiler chicken for the 4 game hens. Use 3 to 4 cups of salt for one chicken in a pot or casserole and bake for about 75 minutes.

Steamed Chicken Breast with Vegetables and Soy Vinaigrette

SERVES 4

SOY VINAIGRETTE

1/3 cup low-sodium soy sauce

1/4 cup rice vinegar

2 tablespoons chopped Maui or other sweet onion

1/2 teaspoon sugar

2 teaspoons olive oil

CHICKEN

1 tablespoon julienned fresh Thai basil

4 boneless chicken breast halves, skin on

1 teaspoon shichimi (see page 28)

1 teaspoon salt

2 stalks lemon grass

12 kaffir lime leaves (see page 35)

1 cup cilantro, including stems, plus sprigs for garnish

SALAD

1 tablespoon olive oil

2 ounces fresh shiitake mushrooms, chopped, about 1 cup

Shichimi (see page 28)

Salt

1 cup chopped cucumber

1 cup chopped tomato

1 tablespoon freshly squeezed lemon juice

A breast of chicken cooks in minutes, making it the ideal quick meal entrée. By steaming it over water and fragrant herbs, I'm infusing a subtle layer of flavor that will be brought forth by the assertive soy sauce dressing. Steaming keeps the chicken moist and succulent while the crunch of cucumbers and the chewiness of shiitake mushrooms engage the senses of the mouth.

To prepare the vinaigrette, in a small bowl whisk together the soy sauce, vinegar, onion, sugar, and olive oil. Set aside.

To prepare the chicken, push the basil leaves under the chicken skin. Season each breast with *shichimi* and salt. Arrange the chicken in a steamer basket.

In the bottom of a steamer, bring water to a boil over high heat. Add the lemon grass, lime leaves, and cilantro. Decrease the heat to achieve a simmer and position the steamer basket over the water. Cover, and steam the chicken for 8 to 10 minutes, until cooked through. Turn off the heat and keep warm.

To prepare the salad, heat the olive oil in a small sauté pan over high heat. Add the mushrooms and sauté for 30 to 45 seconds, until lightly browned. Season the mushrooms with *shichimi* and salt. Transfer the mushrooms to a bowl and add the cucumber and tomato. Pour the vinaigrette over the salad and add the lemon juice. Stir well. Season to taste with *shichimi* and salt and mix well.

Divide the salad among 4 plates and place a chicken breast on each. Garnish with cilantro sprigs and serve immediately.

Pan-Seared Chicken with Honey Sauce, Couscous, and Vegetables

SERVES 4

CHICKEN

1 (3- to 4-pound) chicken
Salt and freshly ground black pepper
2 tablespoons canola oil

HONEY SAUCE

1/4 cup unsalted butter
1 tablespoon freshly cracked black
  pepper
3 tablespoons shallots, minced
3 tablespoons sherry vinegar
1/3 cup honey

1 1/4 cups chicken stock (page 150)
1 cup couscous
4 strips bacon, chopped, about
  1/2 cup
1/4 cup chopped onion
1 tablespoon minced fresh garlic
1 to 2 red chile peppers, julienned
1 cup broccolini, cut into bite-sized
  pieces
1 cup julienned red cabbage
1/2 cup julienned red bell pepper
1 to 2 tablespoons canola oil
Salt and freshly ground black pepper
1 cup micro-greens, for garnish
Olive oil
Freshly squeezed lemon juice

Black pepper, honey, and sherry vinegar are combined in a lively, zesty, sweet-tart sauce that is delicious with this simple chicken preparation. Couscous is tossed together with vegetables to complete the family-style meal.

To prepare the chicken, cut along one side of the breastbone, easing the meat away from the bone in one piece. Continue cutting until the meat is free and you have reached the wing joint. Cut through the wing joint, freeing the meat from the carcass. Trim the wing bone at the first joint. Repeat with the other breast. To remove the legs, twist the leg outward and cut through the joint. With a sharp paring knife, slit the thigh meat to expose the bone. Scrape the meat from the bones and joint to free it. Repeat with the other leg and thigh. Season the chicken with salt and pepper.

Place a heavy sauté pan over medium-high heat and add the oil. Place the chicken pieces in the pan, skin side down. Cook until the skin is crisp and brown, about 5 minutes. Turn the chicken over and cook for another 4 to 5 minutes, until cooked through. Remove the pan from the heat and keep warm.

To prepare the sauce, place a small saucepan over medium-high heat and add the butter. When the butter is melted, add the pepper and shallots and cook for 2 to 3 minutes to infuse the flavors into the butter. Add the vinegar and stir to deglaze the pan, scraping up any browned bits with a wooden spatula. Continue to cook and reduce the liquid for 2 to 3 minutes. Whisk in the honey and simmer for 2 to 3 minutes to blend the flavors. Keep warm until ready to serve.

Place the stock in a saucepan over high heat and bring to a boil. When the stock is boiling, stir in the couscous in a continuous stream. Remove the pan from the heat, cover, and let the couscous steep to cook for about 5 minutes, or until tender.

Heat a sauté pan over high heat. Add the bacon and fry for 2 to 3 minutes, until lightly browned but not crisp. Add the onion and cook for 2 to 3 minutes, until the onion is translucent. Add the garlic and cook for 30 seconds, or until barely light golden brown. Add the chiles, broccolini, cabbage, and bell pepper and toss together. Decrease the heat to medium, cover the pan, and cook for 2 to 3 minutes. When the vegetables are almost cooked, add the couscous and toss together, adding canola oil as necessary to prevent the couscous from sticking to the pan. Season to taste with salt and pepper.

Place the micro-greens in a small bowl and drizzle with a little olive oil and a squeeze of lemon juice. Toss together and add salt and pepper to taste.

To serve, divide the chicken pieces among 4 plates and spoon the vegetables and couscous alongside. Drizzle the sauce over all and top the chicken with the seasoned greens.

Roy's Tips

Serve the honey sauce with duck as prepared in the Roasted Duck Salad with Deep-Fried Tofu and Mango (page 78).

This chicken accompanied by a salad and Pickled Mango Vinaigrette (page 86) will make a simple and delicious meal.

Hawaiian Plate Lunch: Macaroni Salad, Shichimi Chicken, Thai Pineapple Rice, and Barbecue Salmon

SERVES 6

MACARONI SALAD

1 tablespoon plus 1/2 teaspoon salt

4 ounces uncooked macaroni, about 1 cup

1 egg yolk

1 clove garlic

2 teaspoons freshly squeezed lemon juice

2 tablespoons olive oil

6 tablespoons canola oil

4 sweet basil leaves

Freshly ground black pepper

CHICKEN

1 (3-pound) chicken

2 tablespoons finely minced lemon grass

1 tablespoon minced fresh garlic

1 tablespoon minced fresh ginger

1 tablespoon minced shallots

1/2 to 1 tablespoon shichimi (see page 28)

Salt

2 tablespoons canola oil

PINEAPPLE RICE

2 tablespoons canola oil

1/2 cup minced onion

1 teaspoon minced fresh garlic

1 teaspoon minced fresh ginger

1 teaspoon minced lemon grass

(continued)

Locals and frequent visitors often enjoy the Hawaiian "Plate Lunch." Most often this noontime special features two scoops of rice, usually white and sticky, a protein or two, and a scoop of mayonnaise-rich macaroni salad. Typically, an ice cream scoop is used to spoon the rice onto the plate. The plate is traditionally paper, though Styrofoam trays are more common today. Here's my version of a plate lunch full of all the flavors we call "local" in the Islands.

To prepare the macaroni salad, bring 4 quarts of water to a boil in a large saucepan over high heat. Add the 1 tablespoon salt and the macaroni and cook for 8 to 10 minutes, until tender. Drain in a colander, rinse with cool water, and drain again. Transfer to a bowl.

Place the egg yolk, garlic, lemon juice, olive oil, canola oil, basil leaves, and the 1/2 teaspoon salt in a blender and purée until smooth. Add to the macaroni, season with pepper, and mix well. Adjust seasoning with salt if necessary. Refrigerate for at least 2 hours before serving.

To prepare the chicken, rinse and pat dry with paper towels. Place the chicken on a rack in a roasting pan.

In a small bowl, combine the lemon grass, garlic, ginger, shallots, and *shichimi* and mix well. Coat the chicken with the seasonings, placing some of the mixture inside the cavity. Let the chicken stand at room temperature for 30 minutes.

Preheat the oven to 350°F.

Season the chicken with salt and coat with the oil. Place in the oven and roast for 1 hour, or until browned and an instant-read thermometer registers 160°F at the thigh joint. Remove from the oven and allow to cool for 1 hour.

To prepare the rice, place a sauté pan over high heat. Add the oil and when it is hot, add the onion, garlic, ginger, and lemon grass. Sauté for 2 to 3 minutes, until golden brown. Add the pineapple, red bell pepper, yellow bell pepper, and basil and cook for 1 minute, until the peppers are softened.

1 cup diced fresh pineapple

$1/4$ cup diced red bell pepper

$1/4$ cup diced yellow bell pepper

1 tablespoon chopped fresh
  Thai basil

2 cups Thai sticky rice, soaked
  overnight in water (see page 49)

Salt and freshly ground black pepper

SALMON

1 pound salmon fillets

$1/2$ cup hoisin sauce

$1/4$ cup sugar

1 tablespoon minced fresh garlic

1 tablespoon minced fresh ginger

$1/2$ cup soy sauce

$1/3$ cup ko chu jang sauce
  (see page 26)

$1/2$ cup minced green onions

Julienned green onion, for garnish

Transfer the pineapple mixture to a bowl. Drain the uncooked rice, add it to the bowl and mix well. Place the rice mixture in a bamboo rice steamer or a cheesecloth-lined steamer basket.

In the bottom of a steamer, bring water to a boil over high heat. Decrease the heat to achieve a simmer and position the steamer basket over the water. Cover, and steam for 15 to 20 minutes, until the rice is tender. Season with salt and pepper and mix well.

To prepare the salmon, arrange the fillets in a baking dish in 1 layer. In a bowl, combine the hoisin, sugar, garlic, ginger, soy sauce, *ko chu jang* sauce, and green onions and mix well. Spread the mixture over the salmon and marinate for 20 minutes at room temperature.

Prepare a hot fire in a charcoal grill or preheat a gas grill to medium-high. Place the salmon on the grill rack, skin side up, and grill for about 2 minutes, until browned. Turn and cook the salmon another 2 to 3 minutes, until it flakes with slight pressure from a fork.

To serve, divide the macaroni salad, chicken, rice, and salmon among 6 plates. Garnish with green onion and serve immediately.

MediterAsian Saffron Chicken

SERVES 4

SAFFRON CHICKEN

4 boneless, skinless chicken breast
   halves

2 cups chicken stock (page 150)

1 tomato, diced

1 zebra or other sweet tomato, diced

1 tablespoon minced cilantro

1 tablespoon minced fresh thyme

1 tablespoon julienned fresh
   sweet basil

Pinch of saffron

20 ounces firm tofu, drained

Salt and freshly ground black pepper

$1/4$ cup vegetable oil

2 ounces fresh shiitake mushrooms,
   chopped, about 1 cup

2 baby bok choy, tops only

2 teaspoons minced fresh garlic

2 teaspoons minced fresh ginger

4 sprigs thyme, for garnish

Fresh tomatoes and herbs add sparkle to poached chicken breasts in this light dish suggesting the sunny Mediterranean. But underneath is some pan-fried tofu and stir-fried vegetables reminiscent of Asia—a fusion of culinary techniques and flavors.

In a sauté pan, arrange the chicken in 1 layer. Add the stock, tomatoes, cilantro, thyme, basil, and saffron. Cover and bring to a gentle boil over high heat, then decrease the heat to low and simmer for 20 minutes, until the chicken is cooked.

Cut the tofu into 8 ($1/2$-inch-thick) pieces. Drain on paper towels and extract as much moisture as possible. Season with salt and pepper. Heat 2 tablespoons of the oil in a nonstick pan over high heat. Add the tofu and cook, turning once, for 1 minute on each side, until golden brown. Arrange 2 pieces of tofu on each of 4 plates and keep warm.

In the same pan, heat the remaining 2 tablespoons oil over high heat. Add the mushrooms, bok choy, garlic, and ginger and cook for 1 to 2 minutes, until the bok choy is wilted. Season with salt and pepper.

Place the vegetables on top of the tofu. Top with a chicken breast and ladle the cooking liquid around the plate. Garnish with a sprig of thyme and serve immediately.

Thai-Style Deep-fried Mullet with Coconut-Curry Sauce and Pineapple Fried Rice

SERVES 4

SAUCE

2 tablespoons vegetable oil

2 tablespoons minced lemon grass

1 tablespoon minced fresh garlic

1 tablespoon minced fresh ginger

3/4 cup coconut milk

2 teaspoons red Thai curry paste (see page 14)

1 tablespoon palm or light brown sugar

1 tablespoon fish sauce

2 tablespoons julienned Thai basil, plus additional for garnish

RICE

2 tablespoons vegetable oil

2 teaspoons minced fresh garlic

2 teaspoons minced fresh ginger

2 tablespoons minced carrot

2 ounces minced char siu, about 1/2 cup (see page 51)

2 tablespoons minced red bell pepper, plus additional for garnish

2 tablespoons minced yellow bell pepper, plus additional for garnish

2 green onions, minced

1 red chile pepper, minced

1/2 cup finely diced fresh pineapple

2 cups cooked long-grain white rice

2 tablespoons fish sauce

2 tablespoons minced cilantro, plus additional sprigs for garnish

A hint of sweetness will lure your palate into accepting the spiciness of the Thai-style curry sauce that envelops this deep-fried whole fish. The rice is a perfect foil too, with the sweetness and acidity of pineapple playing against the savory but rich sauce. Crunchy vegetables in the rice are a contrast to the moist and soft interior of the fish and the creaminess of the coconut milk sauce.

To prepare the sauce, place a sauté pan over medium-high heat. Add the oil and when it is hot, add the lemon grass, garlic, and ginger and cook for 20 to 30 seconds, until barely light golden brown. Pour in the coconut milk and stir. Add the curry paste, sugar, fish sauce, and basil and blend well with a whisk. When the mixture comes to a boil, decrease the heat to low and simmer for 4 to 5 minutes to blend the flavors. Taste and adjust the seasoning with sugar or fish sauce. Pass the sauce through a fine-meshed sieve and keep warm.

To prepare the rice, heat a wok over high heat. Add the oil and when it is hot, add the garlic and ginger and sauté for 20 to 30 seconds, until barely light golden brown. Add the carrot, *char siu,* red bell pepper, yellow bell pepper, green onions, and chile pepper and stir-fry for 1 to 2 minutes, until the vegetables are softened. Add the pineapple and the rice and stir-fry until warmed through. Add the fish sauce and toss several times to mix well. Taste and adjust the seasoning with salt if necessary. Mix in the cilantro. Remove from the heat and keep warm.

Score the fish by cutting 3 or 4 slits into the flesh on each side. Season both sides of the fish and the cavity with salt and pepper. Coat with flour, shaking off any excess.

Place a large sauté pan over high heat. Pour in the oil to a depth of 3 inches. When the oil is hot, immerse 1 fish in the oil. Fry for 3 to 4 minutes, until brown and crispy. Turn and fry for 3 to 4 minutes on the other side, until brown and crispy. With a slotted spatula, remove from the oil and drain on paper towels. Repeat for the second fish. Transfer both fish to a large serving platter.

FISH

2 (1¹/₂- to 2-pound) mullets or
    pompanos, cleaned

Salt and freshly ground pepper

Flour, for dredging

Canola oil, for deep-frying

Spoon the rice alongside the fish. Ladle the curry sauce over the fish and garnish with basil, red bell pepper, yellow bell pepper, and cilantro sprigs. Serve immediately.

Roy's Tips

To test the temperature of the oil for deep-frying, add a pinch of flour to the oil. If it sizzles vigorously, the oil is hot enough.

The more red Thai curry paste you use, the hotter and saltier the sauce will be. A little more sugar will help to balance the flavors.

For the fried rice, use rice that has been cooked and refrigerated overnight. Long-grain rice is a good choice for this dish because the grains will stay separate; converted rice works well too.

Ponape Pepper–Crusted Shutome on Cassoulet of Offal

SERVES 4

CASSOULET

2 ham hocks

$^1/_2$ pound honeycomb tripe

$^1/_2$ pound pig's stomach

3 pig's feet

2 tablespoons canola oil

1 cup coarsely chopped carrot

1 cup coarsely chopped celery

1 cup coarsely chopped onion

6 tablespoons coarsely chopped fresh garlic

1 tablespoon fresh thyme leaves

8 to 10 cups veal stock (page 156)

2 tablespoons olive oil

10 fresh shiitake mushrooms, sliced

$^1/_2$ cup bottled clam juice

1 cup demi-glace, plus additional for garnish (page 156)

2 tablespoons unsalted butter, chilled

SHUTOME

4 (6-ounce, 1-inch-thick) shutome steaks (see page 38)

1 tablespoon kosher or sea salt

3 tablespoons cracked Ponape peppercorns

$^1/_4$ cup grated lemon zest

2 tablespoons fresh thyme leaves

$^1/_4$ cup canola oil

Thyme sprigs, for garnish

Cassoulet is a traditional French dish of white beans, sausage, duck confit, and other ingredients cooked together in a mouthwatering casserole. This version of cassoulet combines offal—ham hocks, tripe, and pig's feet and stomach—in a stew that is texturally interesting and full of the robust, rich flavors of a traditional cassoulet. The succulent, oil-rich shutome (Hawaiian swordfish) is seasoned with refreshing lemon zest and vibrant, pungent peppercorns from Ponape in Micronesia.

Place the ham hocks, tripe, pig's stomach, and pig's feet in a large saucepan. Add water to cover and place over high heat. Bring to a boil and cook for about 5 minutes to remove the odor and boil off the impurities, skimming off the foam and impurities as they rise to the top. Remove from the heat and drain in a colander. Rinse the offal under running water. Transfer to a bowl of ice water to soak for 30 minutes.

Place a large saucepan over high heat. Add the canola oil and when it is hot, add the carrot, celery, and onion. Cook for 3 to 4 minutes, until brown. Add 4 tablespoons of the garlic and cook for 30 seconds, or until barely light golden brown. Drain the offal and add to the pan along with the thyme and veal stock. Bring to a boil, then decrease the heat to low and simmer for 3 to 4 hours, until the offal is tender, adding more veal stock or water as needed to keep the offal covered in liquid. Drain the offal and allow to cool. Cut the meat off the ham hocks and pig's feet and chop into bite-sized pieces. Slice the tripe and stomach into strips.

Place a large saucepan over high heat and add the olive oil. When the oil is hot, add the remaining 2 tablespoons garlic and the mushrooms and sauté for 30 to 45 seconds, until lightly browned. Add the clam juice, demi-glace, and the offal. Bring to a boil, then decrease the heat to medium and simmer for 5 minutes to blend the flavors and thicken the liquid. Taste and adjust seasoning with salt if necessary. Whisk in the butter and keep warm.

To prepare the *shutome,* coat both sides of the fish with the salt, peppercorns, lemon zest, and thyme. Rub in the oil. Heat a sauté pan over medium-high heat and add the *shutome.* Sear for 3 to 4 minutes, until brown and crisp. Turn and sear the other side for 3 to 4 minutes, until the flesh flakes with slight pressure from a fork.

Divide the cassoulet among 4 deep plates and top with the *shutome.* Drizzle with demi-glace, garnish with thyme sprigs, and serve immediately.

Roy's Tips

The cassoulet should be started the day before you want to serve it.

Offal is often found in Chinatown markets or can be ordered through a butcher.

Ponape peppercorns are not easily found and can be substituted with Tellicherry or other pungent black peppercorns. To crack the black peppercorns, place them in a plastic bag and pound them with a meat pounder, mallet, or hammer.

Mahimahi with Citrus Sauce, Apple Bananas, and Macadamia Nuts

SERVES 4

CITRUS SAUCE

3/4 cup water

1/3 cup sugar

1 tablespoon freshly crushed black peppercorns

2 tablespoons honey

2 teaspoons grated orange zest

2 teaspoons grated lemon zest

3 tablespoons orange juice concentrate

1 tablespoon freshly squeezed lemon juice

3 tablespoons passion fruit syrup (see page 18)

2 teaspoons canola oil

BANANAS

2 apple bananas (see page 18)

1/4 teaspoon shichimi (see page 28)

2 tablespoons sweetened coconut flakes

1 tablespoon canola oil

4 (6-ounce) mahimahi fillets

Salt

1 tablespoon canola oil

2 cups mesclun

1 cup julienned cucumber, for garnish

6 tablespoons chopped macadamia nuts, for garnish

Mahimahi is one of Hawaii's most popular fish; firm-fleshed and mild-flavored, it can be cooked in almost any manner and cloaked in almost any sauce. I like the flavor of citrus with mahimahi, enhanced by some spicy peppercorns. Sweet bananas, a hint of coconut, and macadamia nuts add to the tropical flavors in this light dish.

To prepare the sauce, in a saucepan, combine the water, sugar, and peppercorns. Bring to a boil over high heat, decrease the heat to medium, and simmer for 10 to 15 minutes, until the sauce becomes syrupy. Add the honey, orange zest, lemon zest, orange juice concentrate, lemon juice, syrup, and canola oil. Continue to simmer for 10 to 15 minutes, until the sauce is syrupy and reduced by one-third. Pass through a fine-meshed sieve and keep warm.

Split the bananas in half lengthwise. Combine the *shichimi* and coconut flakes in a shallow bowl. Coat the cut side of each banana piece with the coconut mixture. Place a small sauté pan over medium heat and add the oil. When the oil is hot, add the bananas, coconut side down. Cook for about 2 minutes, or until golden brown. Turn and cook the other side for 1 minute, or until lightly browned. Remove from the heat and keep warm.

Season the mahimahi with salt. Place a sauté pan over high heat and add the oil. When the oil is hot, add the mahimahi. Cook for 2 minutes, or until browned. Turn and cook the other side for 2 minutes, or until the flesh flakes with slight pressure from a fork.

To serve, divide the greens among 4 plates. Place the mahimahi on top of the greens and the banana on top of the mahimahi. Drizzle 3 to 4 tablespoons of the sauce around each serving. Garnish with the cucumber and macadamia nuts. Serve immediately.

Roy's Tip

Passion fruit syrup is available in some Hawaiian stores. If you cannot find it substitute with passion fruit juice concentrate or 2 more tablespoons of orange juice concentrate.

Lemon Grass–Crusted Hawaiian Shutome and Thai Peanut Sauce

SERVES 4

SAUCE

1 cup coconut milk

1/3 cup firmly packed brown sugar

1/4 cup soy sauce

1 tablespoon fish sauce

2 teaspoons mushroom soy sauce
(see page 16)

1/4 cup chopped Maui or other
sweet onions

2 teaspoons massaman curry paste
(see page 27)

2 tablespoons chopped cilantro

5 tablespoons creamy peanut butter

2 teaspoons rice vinegar

1 tablespoon freshly squeezed
lemon juice

1 kaffir lime leaf, finely chopped
(see page 35)

2 tablespoons chopped fresh
Thai basil

1 teaspoon minced fresh garlic

1 teaspoon minced fresh ginger

SHUTOME

4 (6-ounce, 1-inch-thick) shutome or
shark steaks (see page 38)

Salt

2 tablespoons minced lemon grass

1 tablespoon minced fresh garlic

1 tablespoon minced fresh ginger

1 tablespoon minced shallots

1 teaspoon shichimi (see page 28)

3 tablespoons canola oil

Kaiware, for garnish (see page 41)

Gari, for garnish (see page 22)

Shutome (Hawaiian swordfish) has a robust flavor and an oiliness that keeps it moist—it's one of my favorite fish. Because it is so hearty, it can pair with assertive seasonings like lemon grass, garlic, ginger, and shichimi. And if that's not enough to get your taste buds excited, a spicy Thai peanut sauce will do the trick—thick, rich, and zesty. This dish doesn't need much else except some steamed jasmine rice to soak up the sauce.

To prepare the sauce, combine all the ingredients in a saucepan, blending with a whisk. Place the saucepan over medium-high heat and bring to a boil. Decrease the heat to low and simmer for 30 minutes, or until the oil from the curry paste rises to the surface. Pass through a fine-meshed sieve and keep warm.

Season the *shutome* on both sides with salt. In a small bowl, combine the lemon grass, garlic, ginger, shallots, and *shichimi.* Spread the mixture over 1 side of each piece of fish. Let stand for 5 minutes.

Heat a nonstick sauté pan over medium-high heat. Pour the oil over the *shutome.* Place in the pan, crust side down, and cook for 3 minutes, or until the crust is golden brown. Turn and cook the other side for 3 minutes, or until the flesh flakes with slight pressure from a fork.

Place a *shutome* steak on each of 4 plates, crust side up. Ladle the sauce around and garnish with *kaiware* and *gari.*

Roy's Tip

The peanut sauce would make a fine accompaniment to the Spicy Chicken Wings (page 66) or serve it with strips of fried tofu.

Chinese-Style Whole Steamed Fish

SERVES 4

SAUCE

1/4 cup peanut oil

6 cloves garlic

6 (1/2-inch) chunks fresh ginger, unpeeled

2 green onions, chopped into 1-inch pieces

2 to 3 whole red chile peppers

1/2 cup reduced-sodium soy sauce

1/4 cup cilantro leaves

2 tablespoons sugar

FISH

1 (2-pound) whole uhu, snapper, or rock cod, scaled and cleaned (see page 38)

1/4 cup julienned fresh ginger

6 tablespoons cilantro leaves

6 tablespoons julienned green onion

1 tablespoon vegetable oil

8 heads baby bok choy

1/2 cup peanut oil

2 tablespoons shallot oil (page 153)

1/4 cup thinly sliced red bell pepper

1/4 cup thinly sliced yellow bell pepper

A traditional Chinese steamed fish is dressed with soy sauce and hot oil as it emerges from the steamer. In this recipe, the soy sauce is infused with the flavors of garlic, ginger, green onion, and chile peppers, adding an aromatic and vibrant dimension to the sauce. Because this mixture is poured directly onto the delicate white fish, I prefer using a reduced-sodium soy sauce, less sharp but full of flavor, especially with all the added ingredients. Steamed short-grain white rice is a natural accompaniment to this dish.

To prepare the sauce, place a small saucepan over medium-high heat. Add the oil and when it is smoking, add the garlic, then the ginger, then the green onions, and then the chile peppers, stirring occasionally, allowing the oil to reheat after each addition. Decrease the heat to low and cook for 8 to 10 minutes, stirring occasionally, until golden brown and caramelized.

Add the soy sauce, cilantro, and sugar and slowly bring to a boil. Taste and adjust seasoning, adding more sugar if necessary. Remove from the heat, pour through a fine-meshed sieve, and set aside.

Score the fish by cutting 3 or 4 diagonal slits into the flesh on each side. Place 1 tablespoon of the ginger, 2 tablespoons of the cilantro, and 2 tablespoons of the green onion in the cavity of the fish.

Arrange the fish on a steaming rack and top with 1 tablespoon of the ginger, 2 tablespoons of the cilantro, and 2 tablespoons of the green onion.

In the bottom of a steamer, bring water to a boil over high heat. Decrease the heat to achieve a simmer and position the steaming rack over the water. Cover and steam the fish for 8 minutes per inch of thickness, or until the flesh flakes with slight pressure from a fork.

Place a sauté pan over high heat. Add the vegetable oil and when it is hot, add the bok choy. Sauté for 2 to 3 minutes, until wilted. Transfer to a large serving platter and keep warm.

Heat the peanut oil in a saucepan over high heat until smoking. Keep hot.

Remove the fish from the steamer and transfer to the serving platter with the bok choy. Pour the sauce over the fish and drizzle the shallot oil over. Arrange the remaining 2 tablespoons ginger, 2 tablespoons green onion, red bell pepper, and yellow bell pepper on top of the fish. Pour the peanut oil over; it will sizzle as you pour. Garnish with the remaining 2 tablespoons cilantro and serve immediately.

Steamed Opakapaka and Salmon with Shrimp Mousse

SERVES 4

SHRIMP MOUSSE

12 medium shrimp, peeled, deveined, and without tails

$1/8$ teaspoon salt

$1/8$ teaspoon freshly ground white pepper

$1/4$ cup loosely packed fresh sweet basil leaves

1 tablespoon unsalted butter

1 egg

$1/3$ cup cream

4 (3-ounce) thin salmon fillets

4 (3-ounce) thin opakapaka fillets (see page 38)

Salt

$1/2$ teaspoon shichimi (see page 28)

3 tablespoons minced pancetta

1 ounce fresh shiitake mushrooms, sliced thin, about $1/2$ cup

1 tablespoon julienned fresh ginger

1 cup julienned green onion

3 tablespoons soy sauce

2 tablespoons sesame oil

1 cup fish stock (page 154)

A savory shrimp mousse forms the filling for this fish "sandwich" featuring oily, rich salmon and delicate opakapaka, *Hawaii's pink snapper. All of the elements retain their moisture through the steaming process, with vapors enhanced with pancetta, mushrooms, ginger, and fish stock to add another dimension of flavor.*

To prepare the mousse, place the shrimp in a food processor and chop until puréed and smooth. Add the salt, pepper, basil, butter, and egg and continue to process until smooth. With the motor running, slowly add the cream. Transfer the mousse to a bowl.

Season the salmon and *opakapaka* fillets with salt. Spread one-fourth of the mousse onto each salmon fillet. Place the *opakapaka* fillets on top, forming 4 sandwiches. Fill in the sides with the mousse to form a compact shape.

Sprinkle the *opakapaka* with *shichimi.* Place the fish sandwiches in a shallow bowl. Sprinkle the pancetta, mushrooms, ginger, and green onion around and on top of the fish. Drizzle the soy sauce and sesame oil over the fish and add the fish stock. Place the bowl on a steaming rack.

In the bottom of a steamer, bring water to a boil over high heat. Decrease the heat to achieve a simmer and position the steaming rack over the water. Cover and steam for 10 to 12 minutes, until the flesh flakes with slight pressure from a fork. Remove from the steamer and serve immediately.

Roy's Tip

Serve this dish with cooked short-grain white rice and stir-fried bok choy.

Golden Shrimp-Stuffed Tofu

SERVES 4 TO 6

SAUCE

1 cup chicken stock (page 150)

1 tablespoon oyster sauce

1 tablespoon cornstarch

1 tablespoon water

14 ounces firm tofu

2¼ teaspoons salt

6 medium shrimp, peeled, deveined, and without tails

1 egg white

Pinch of freshly ground white pepper

1 teaspoon sesame oil

1 teaspoon cornstarch

3 cups vegetable oil, for deep-frying

Green leaf lettuce leaves

2 tablespoons thinly sliced green onion, for garnish

Cookbook author, chef, and restaurateur Leann Chin of Minnesota was a guest on Hawaii Cooks with Roy Yamaguchi *in a special show about Chinese New Year celebrations. She prepared this dish of golden fried tofu, chewy and savory, that resembles bricks of gold, a symbolic wish for prosperity in the New Year.*

To prepare the sauce, in a small saucepan over high heat, combine the chicken stock and oyster sauce. Bring to a boil. In a small bowl, combine the cornstarch and water and mix well. Add the cornstarch mixture to the pan and stir for about 1 minute, until thickened. Remove from the heat and keep warm.

Cut the tofu into 1½ by 1½ by ¾-inch pieces. Scoop out 1 teaspoon of the tofu from the center of each square, and reserve. Place the tofu squares on paper towels to drain excess moisture.

Place 2 cups of warm water in a bowl, add 2 teaspoons of the salt, and stir to dissolve the salt. Place the shrimp in the water and soak for 5 minutes. Drain, rinse the shrimp with cold water, and pat dry with a towel to remove excess water.

Place the shrimp in a food processor with the remaining ¼ teaspoon salt, egg white, pepper, sesame oil, and cornstarch. Process to a smooth paste. Transfer to a bowl and mix with half of the reserved tofu; save the remaining tofu for another use. Place a teaspoon of the mixture in each square of tofu.

Place a wok over high heat and pour in the oil. When the oil is hot (350°F), add the tofu pieces one at a time to prevent them from sticking together. Fry in batches for 2 to 3 minutes, until golden brown. Remove from the oil and drain on paper towels.

Arrange the lettuce leaves on a platter. Place the tofu on the leaves and spoon the sauce over the tofu. Sprinkle with green onion and serve immediately.

Fresh Pasta with Shrimp, Pancetta, Anchovy, and Garlic

SERVES 6

FRESH LINGUINE

2 cups unbleached all-purpose flour

2 eggs

3 to 4 tablespoons water

SAUCE

3 tablespoons olive oil

$^1/_4$ cup diced pancetta

24 large shrimp, peeled and
deveined

2 tablespoons minced anchovy

1 tablespoon minced fresh garlic

2 to 3 shallots, minced, about $^1/_4$ cup

1 cup bottled clam juice

2 cups basic tomato sauce (page 155)

2 tablespoons julienned sweet basil,
plus additional for garnish

2 tablespoons chopped green onion

Freshly ground pepper

This rich, thick pasta sauce relies on anchovies, pancetta, and clam juice for its salty savoriness. To enhance the depth of flavor, I use a fresh tomato sauce and reduce it to a thick but smooth texture. Fresh pasta—egg rich and light—can't be beat in this preparation.

To prepare the linguine, place the flour and eggs in a food processor. Pulse to combine. With the motor running, add the water, a little at a time, until the mixture becomes sticky and begins to form a ball. Remove the dough from the work bowl, cover with plastic wrap, and allow to rest for at least 30 minutes.

Lightly flour 2 baking sheets. Cut the dough into 4 equal pieces and sprinkle each with flour. Pass 1 portion of the dough through the rollers of a hand-cranked pasta machine at the widest setting. Repeat several times at the widest setting, until uniform in thickness. Pass the dough through 2 or 3 successively thinner roller settings to desired thickness. Repeat until all of the dough is rolled to desired thickness. Pass the pasta sheets through the cutter. Spread the cut pasta on the baking sheets.

Bring a large pot of water to a boil over high heat. Add 1 tablespoon of salt and the pasta. Cook for 2 to 3 minutes, until tender. Drain in a colander, reserving a little of the cooking liquid.

To prepare the sauce, place a large sauté pan over high heat. Add 1 tablespoon of the olive oil. Add the pancetta and sauté for 2 minutes, or until almost crisp. Add the shrimp and cook for 1 minute, or until the color begins to change. Add the anchovy and mix with the shrimp for 1 minute, until the shrimp is almost cooked through. Remove the shrimp from the pan, leaving behind the pancetta.

Add the remaining 2 tablespoons olive oil to the pan. Add the garlic and shallots and sauté for 2 minutes, or until lightly browned. Pour in the clam juice, bring to a boil, and cook for about 5 minutes, until reduced by half. Mix in the tomato sauce, basil, and green onion, decrease the heat to low, and simmer for 4 to 5 minutes to blend the flavors.

Return the shrimp to the pan and add the cooked pasta. Mix well and toss together for 3 to 4 minutes, coating the pasta with the sauce.

Season with pepper. If the pasta looks dry, add some of the reserved pasta water.

Transfer to individual pasta bowls or a large serving bowl. Garnish with basil and serve immediately.

Roy's Tips

If you are not making fresh linguine, substitute a pound of dried linguine.

Pasta should always be cooked in a large amount of water. Salt should be added to the pasta water for additional flavor.

It is important to cook the pasta with the sauce, allowing the flavor of the sauce to permeate the pasta.

Vietnamese-Style Cold Udon with Shrimp

SERVES 4

1 pound fresh udon (see page 48)

3 tablespoons minced fresh garlic

2 tablespoons minced fresh ginger

3 tablespoons minced lemon grass

$^1/_4$ cup julienned mint

$^1/_4$ cup plus 1 tablespoon fish sauce

1 to 2 teaspoons shichimi
(see page 28)

24 jumbo shrimp, peeled and
deveined

3 tablespoons vegetable oil

2 ounces fresh shiitake mushrooms,
thinly sliced, about 1 cup

$^1/_4$ cup dried black mushrooms,
soaked in water and julienned
(see page 42)

1 cup julienned carrots

$^1/_4$ cup minced kaffir lime leaf
(see page 35)

$^1/_4$ cup minced cilantro

$^1/_4$ cup julienned Thai basil

$^1/_2$ cup chopped green onion

SALAD

2 cups julienned cucumber

$^1/_2$ cup sliced red bell pepper

$^1/_2$ cup sliced yellow bell pepper

2 tablespoons julienned mint

1 teaspoon white sesame seeds

1 teaspoon black sesame seeds

Fish sauce

Shichimi (see page 28)

In Vietnam, thin rice noodles are served with savory grilled meats or seafood and raw vegetables, a delightful combination of flavors and textures. In this dish, I've chosen thick Japanese udon to stir-fry with vegetables and herbs, topped with spicy shrimp and crunchy vegetables, all flavored with traditional Vietnamese seasonings.

Bring a large pot of water to a boil over high heat. Add the noodles and cook for 2 to 3 minutes, until tender. Drain in a colander and set aside.

In a bowl, combine 1 tablespoon of the garlic, 1 tablespoon of the ginger, 2 tablespoons of the lemon grass, the mint, the $^1/_4$ cup fish sauce, and the *shichimi* and mix well. Add the shrimp and toss well to coat.

Place a wok over high heat and add 1 tablespoon of the oil. When the oil is hot, add the shrimp and sauté for 2 to 3 minutes, until pink and cooked through. Remove from the wok and keep warm.

Return the wok to high heat and add the remaining 2 tablespoons oil. When the oil is hot, add the shiitake mushrooms, black mushrooms, and carrot and cook for 2 minutes, until the shiitake mushrooms are lightly browned. Make a well in the mixture and add the remaining 2 tablespoons garlic and 1 tablespoon ginger. Stir-fry for 20 to 30 seconds, adding more oil if necessary, until barely light golden brown. Add the remaining 1 tablespoon lemon grass and the lime leaf to the well and cook for 30 seconds, until aromatic. Toss the seasonings with the mushrooms and carrot, mixing well. Add the cilantro, basil, green onion, and the 1 tablespoon fish sauce and mix well. Add the noodles and toss together. Taste and adjust the seasoning with fish sauce if necessary to season the noodles. Stir-fry for 1 minute, or until the noodles are warmed through. Remove from the heat.

To prepare the salad, in a bowl, combine the cucumber, red bell pepper, yellow bell pepper, and mint and mix well. Sprinkle with the white and black sesame seeds. Season with fish sauce and *shichimi* and mix well.

Divide the udon mixture among 4 plates. Arrange the shrimp around the udon and top with the salad mixture. Serve immediately.

Shrimp and Clam Linguine with Chile, Lemon Grass, and Black Bean Sauce

SERVES 4

2 tablespoons salt

1 pound linguine

2 tablespoons vegetable oil

16 large shrimp, peeled and deveined

20 Manila or other small clams, scrubbed

2 teaspoons minced fresh garlic

2 teaspoons minced fresh ginger

1/4 cup diced onion

2 stalks lemon grass, sliced, about 1/4 cup

4 teaspoons fermented black beans, rinsed and drained (see page 13)

1/4 cup sherry

2 to 3 tablespoons sriracha or other chile sauce (see page 26)

1/2 pound snow peas, about 1 cup

1/2 cup diced tomato

3 green onions, chopped

1/4 cup chicken stock (page 150)

3/4 cup unsalted butter, cut into pieces

Freshly ground black pepper

Chef de Cuisine Lance Kosaka of Alan Wong's Restaurant is among the next generation of star chefs in Hawaii. As a guest on Hawaii Cooks with Roy Yamaguchi, *he shared this recipe, which he learned from his mentor chef, Alan Wong. In this dish, he tempers the sharp flavors of garlic, ginger, fermented black beans, and* sriracha *with the citrusy notes of lemon grass and the silkiness of butter.*

Bring a large pot of water to a boil over high heat. Add the salt and linguine and cook for 8 to 10 minutes, until tender. Drain in a colander.

Place a large sauté pan over high heat and add the oil. When the oil is hot, add the shrimp and clams and sear for 1 minute. Add the garlic, ginger, onion, lemon grass, and black beans and sauté for 1 to 2 minutes, until aromatic. Pour in the sherry to deglaze the pan, scraping up any browned bits with a wooden spatula. Add the *sriracha,* snow peas, tomato, green onions, stock, and butter and mix until the butter melts.

Add the cooked pasta, mixing to coat with the seasonings. Cover and simmer for 2 to 3 minutes, until the seafood is fully cooked and the butter is melted. Season with salt and pepper to taste and add more chile sauce if desired. Serve immediately on a large platter or in individual bowls.

Tea-Infused Shrimp Sauté

SERVES 4

1 cup water

1 tablespoon green tea leaves
  (see page 34)

3 egg whites

3 tablespoons cornstarch

$1/2$ cup cooking sherry

1 pound medium shrimp, peeled,
  deveined, and butterflied

6 tablespoons peanut oil

1 cup thinly sliced carrot

2 ounces fresh shiitake mushrooms,
  quartered, about 1 cup

4 ounces whole button mushrooms,
  about 1 cup

$1^1/2$ pounds bite-sized broccoli florets,
  about 3 cups

6 green onions, diagonally sliced

$1/2$ onion, sliced

Salt

Green tea leaves, steeped in hot water, are the unusual flavor component in this dish. The tea becomes the basis for the sauce and the leaves are used like an herb to season the shrimp. This is a subtly flavored dish, quite different from my usual bold statements. Steamed white short-grain rice would be a nice accompaniment.

In a small saucepan, heat the water to just below boiling, about 180°F. Remove the pan from the heat, add the tea leaves, and steep for 3 to 4 minutes, until light green. Drain into a small bowl, capturing the liquid and reserving the leaves. When the leaves are cool, mince and set aside.

Place the egg whites in a large bowl and whip for 3 minutes, or until white and frothy. Add the cornstarch and sherry and mix well. Add the shrimp and marinate for 5 minutes.

Place a sauté pan over medium-high heat. Add 3 tablespoons of the oil and when it is hot, add the carrot, shiitake mushrooms, button mushrooms, broccoli, green onions, and sliced onion. Decrease the heat to medium and sauté for 3 to 4 minutes, until cooked but not brown. Season with salt to taste. Transfer to a serving platter and keep warm.

In the same sauté pan over medium-low heat, heat the remaining 3 tablespoons oil. When the oil is hot, add the shrimp, adjusting the heat to prevent browning. Cook for 2 to 3 minutes, until the shrimp start to turn pink. Sprinkle in the tea leaves and lightly toss together. Add the tea liquid and mix well. Continue to cook for 2 to 3 minutes, until the sauce is thickened. Transfer the shrimp to the serving platter and pour the sauce over. Serve immediately.

Shrimp Risotto

SERVES 4

24 large shrimp, peeled and
deveined

Salt and freshly ground black pepper

1/4 cup olive oil

1/2 cup diced onion

1/2 cup diced button mushrooms

2 cups Arborio rice

About 8 cups shrimp stock, heated
(page 154)

1 1/2 ounces fresh shiitake mushrooms,
sliced, about 3/4 cup

1/2 cup fresh peas

1/2 cup fresh fava beans

2 tablespoons julienned fresh
sweet basil

2/3 cup shredded Parmesan cheese

2 tablespoons unsalted butter

1 cup mizuna, for garnish
(see page 42)

1 cup oak leaf lettuce, for garnish

The soft, creamy richness of risotto comes from starchy Arborio rice. Tender, earthy mushrooms, snappy peas and beans, and crunchy pan-fried shrimp are part of the playful textures and savory flavors that make this dish a meal in itself.

Season the shrimp with salt and pepper and coat with 2 tablespoons of the oil. Place a sauté pan over high heat. Add the shrimp to the pan and sauté for 2 to 3 minutes, until cooked through. Transfer to a plate and keep warm.

In the same sauté pan, heat the remaining 2 tablespoons oil over medium-high heat. Add the onion and button mushrooms and cook for 2 to 3 minutes, until the onions are translucent. Add the rice and stir to coat with the oil. Add 2 cups of the hot stock and cook, stirring continuously, until the liquid is absorbed. Continue stirring and adding the stock a cup at a time, until the mixture is creamy and the rice is almost cooked through, about 20 minutes.

Add the shiitake mushrooms, peas, fava beans, and basil and mix well. Add another cup of stock and cook for 1 to 2 minutes, until the liquid is absorbed and the rice is creamy. Test the rice for doneness: the kernels should be soft all the way through but not mushy. Add the cheese and mix to melt and incorporate into the rice. Add the butter and salt and pepper to taste, and stir well.

Spoon the risotto into 4 shallow bowls. Arrange the shrimp on top of the rice and garnish with mizuna and lettuce. Serve immediately.

Roy's Tip

Shelled edamame (see page 41) can be substituted for the fava beans.

Crab with Vanilla Sauce

SERVES 4

2 (3- to 4-pound) live Dungeness crabs

3 tablespoons unsalted butter

2 tablespoons minced shallots

1 whole vanilla bean

1 cup Sauternes or other sweet white wine

1 1/2 cups heavy cream

1/2 teaspoon salt

Fresh chopped chives, for garnish

Chervil sprigs, for garnish

Vanilla, the dried pod of an orchid plant, is primarily used in desserts and pastries. But its flowery flavor and aroma have a place in savory preparations too. Its light essence combined with the richness of cream is a perfect marriage; with crab or lobster it is even more luxurious. Use the whole bean, splitting it and scraping out the miniscule seeds that contain the flavor. In Hawaii, the cultivation of vanilla orchids has become a small industry. Farmers hand pollinate the flowers during annual blooms, and a green bean forms eight to nine months later. The beans are picked and then dried in the sun or by water blanching. The beans turn brown but remain pliable, fragrant, and full of flavor.

Place the crabs in a large pot with 2 to 3 cups of water. Cover, place the pot over high heat, and bring to a boil. Cook for 12 to 15 minutes, until the crabs are red and cooked through. Drain and allow to cool.

When the crabs are cool enough to handle, break off the legs and pincers and crack the shells. Open the top shell, remove the gills, and cut the body into 4 pieces. Arrange all the pieces on a serving platter and keep warm.

Heat a small saucepan over medium-high heat. Add 1 1/2 tablespoons of the butter and when it is melted, add the shallots and cook for about 2 minutes, or until translucent.

With a small knife, split the vanilla bean in half lengthwise and scrape out the seeds. Add the seeds and bean to the pan and sauté for 2 minutes to blend the flavors. Pour in the wine and bring to a boil. Decrease the heat to medium and simmer for 3 to 4 minutes, until the wine is reduced by half. Add the cream and stir well. Just before the mixture returns to a boil, decrease the heat to medium-low and simmer for 3 to 5 minutes, until the sauce thickens enough to coat the back of a spoon. Whisk in the remaining 1 1/2 tablespoons butter and the salt.

Spoon the sauce over the crab and sprinkle with chopped chives. Garnish with sprigs of chervil and serve immediately.

Roy's Tip

For some even richer presentations, the crabmeat can be tossed with the vanilla sauce and served over roast chicken, a medallion of pork, or sautéed spinach and garlic.

Hawaiian Cioppino and Crostini with Eastern Rouille

SERVES 6

ARTICHOKE GARNISH

2 artichokes

Juice of 1 lemon

Oil, for deep-frying

CROSTINI AND ROUILLE

1 fresh baguette

1 to 2 cloves garlic, finely minced

$^1/_3$ cup olive oil

$^2/_3$ cup mayonnaise

2 to 3 tablespoons sambal oelek or sriracha (see page 26)

CIOPPINO

$^1/_4$ cup olive oil

3 tablespoons minced fresh garlic

1 cup white wine

2 tablespoons minced sweet basil

1 tablespoon minced fresh thyme

$^1/_4$ cup minced fresh parsley

1 cup chicken stock (page 150)

1 cup bottled clam juice

4 ripe red tomatoes, chopped, about 2 cups

1 (1$^1/_2$-pound) live Kona crab (see page 37)

2 small whole fish such as mempachi, cleaned (see page 38)

12 to 15 Manila or other small clams, scrubbed

$^1/_2$ pound octopus, cut into bite-sized pieces

12 to 15 fresh mussels, scrubbed

2 ears of corn, each cut into 4 pieces

(continued)

Cioppino, the San Francisco-Italian version of the classic French bouillabaisse without the saffron, is the perfect dish for a family gathering because it will feed a crowd. Have plenty of crostini—garlicky toasted bread—to soak up the delicious broth. But don't forget the rouille: my version of this Provençal sauce combines mayonnaise and chile peppers in a spicy Eastern variation.

To prepare the artichoke garnish, remove the leaves of the artichoke with a knife, trimming down to the fuzzy choke but leaving the stem. Scoop out the choke, exposing the heart. Slice the heart vertically into 4 or 5 pieces, cutting through the heart to the bottom of the stem. Sprinkle the trimmed artichoke with lemon juice to prevent discoloring.

In a small saucepan, heat 3 to 4 inches of oil over high heat. Pat the artichoke pieces dry. When the oil is hot, add the artichoke pieces, a few at a time and fry for 3 to 4 minutes, until golden brown and cooked through. Remove from the oil and drain on paper towels. Keep warm.

To prepare the crostini, preheat the oven to 400°F.

Cut the baguette into thin rounds or diagonal slices and place on a baking sheet in 1 layer. In a small bowl, mix together the garlic and oil and brush onto the bread slices. Place in the oven and toast for 8 to 10 minutes, until crisp. Remove from the oven and set aside.

In a small bowl, combine the mayonnaise and *sambal oelek.* Cover and refrigerate the rouille until ready to serve.

To prepare the cioppino, place a very large wide saucepan over medium heat. Add the olive oil and when it is hot, add the garlic and sauté for 20 to 30 seconds, until cooked but not brown. Increase the heat to high, pour in the white wine, and bring to a boil. Add the basil, thyme, and parsley and continue to boil for 2 to 3 minutes, until the liquid is reduced by about half. Add the stock, clam juice, and tomatoes, and bring to a boil for 2 to 3 minutes, until the tomatoes are soft and the flavors blend.

Plunge the crab into the boiling broth and cover for 1 minute. Uncover and add the fish, clams, octopus, mussels, and corn to the pan. Spoon the broth over the seafood as it cooks to absorb the flavors. Cook for 3 to 4 minutes, then add the shrimp, scallops, and squid. Cook for 3 to 4 minutes, until all the seafood is cooked through.

1/2 pound medium Kauai shrimp with heads, unpeeled, rinsed and drained (see page 37)

10 to 12 large scallops, rinsed and drained

1/2 pound squid, cleaned and cut into bite-sized pieces

Transfer the seafood and corn to a large platter and keep warm. Continue to cook the broth for 3 to 4 minutes, until reduced by one-third. Taste and adjust the seasoning with salt if necessary.

To serve, cut the crab and fish into serving-sized pieces. Divide the seafood among 6 wide bowls and ladle in the broth. Garnish with the artichokes. Serve immediately with the crostini and rouille on the side.

Roy's Tips

Dungeness crab can be substituted for Kona crab.

For easier eating, steam the crab for 5 minutes (it doesn't have to be cooked completely), cool, then clean, and break into pieces (save any juice to add to the broth). Add the cleaned crab pieces to the stew with the shrimp and scallops so it can cook through and absorb the flavors.

You don't have to use all the seafood listed here: just be sure that whatever you select is as fresh as possible.

Kona Cold Lobster with Spicy Mango Sauce

SERVES 4

SAUCE

2 ripe mangoes

3/4 cup rice vinegar

2 green onions, roughly chopped

3 sprigs cilantro

2 kaffir lime leaves, finely chopped
(see page 35)

2 teaspoons minced lemon grass

2 teaspoons minced fresh garlic

2 teaspoons minced fresh ginger

1/2 cup sugar

1 tablespoon Lingham chile sauce or
other sweet chile sauce

4 (1 1/2-pound) live Kona cold lobsters
(see page 37)

1/4 cup macadamia nut oil

2 tablespoons vegetable oil

1 cup julienned red bell pepper

2 ounces fresh shiitake mushrooms,
sliced, about 1 cup

12 asparagus spears, cut into 1-inch
pieces

1/4 cup oyster sauce

Cilantro sprigs, for garnish

A tart and zesty mango sauce will awaken your taste buds as you delve into delicate fresh lobster meat. The combination will no doubt make you appreciate the subtly flavored vegetables on the side.

To prepare the sauce, peel and seed the mangoes, saving the pits. Cut the mango into 1/4-inch dice and set aside.

Combine the mango pits, vinegar, green onions, cilantro, lime leaves, lemon grass, garlic, ginger, sugar, and chile sauce in a saucepan. Bring to a boil over high heat. Decrease the heat to medium and simmer for 15 to 20 minutes, until the sauce is reduced by one-third. Pass through a fine-meshed sieve and stir in the diced mango. Keep warm.

To prepare the lobsters, bring a very large pot of water to a boil over high heat. Plunge the lobsters into the water, cover, and cook for 5 minutes. Remove from the water and allow to cool. Break the lobsters into tail, claw, and leg sections and set aside.

Place a large sauté pan over high heat and add the macadamia nut oil. When the oil is hot, add the lobster sections and sauté for 2 minutes, or until cooked through. Keep warm.

In the same sauté pan over high heat, add the vegetable oil. When the oil is hot, add the bell pepper, mushrooms, and asparagus. Sauté for 2 minutes, or until the vegetables are crisp-tender. Add the oyster sauce and stir to mix.

To serve, divide the vegetables and lobster among 4 plates. Drizzle the mango sauce over the lobster. Garnish with cilantro and serve immediately.

Stir-Fried Lobster with Spicy Garlic and Black Pepper Sauce

SERVES 4

1 pound choy sum (see page 40)

1/2 pound asparagus

2 tablespoons salt

4 (1¼-pound) live Kona cold lobsters (see page 37)

4 cups vegetable oil

4 cloves garlic, crushed

2 stalks lemon grass, finely chopped

4 kaffir lime leaves (see page 35)

1 teaspoon chile garlic sauce

1 shallot, finely chopped

1 tablespoon freshly crushed black peppercorns

1/4 cup brandy

1 cup chicken stock (page 150)

2 tablespoons soy sauce

Fish sauce

1 tablespoon cornstarch

2 tablespoons water

Juice of 1 lemon

4 green onions, sliced

5 sprigs cilantro, chopped

Chef Wayne Hirabayashi, executive chef of the Kahala Mandarin Oriental hotel in Honolulu, learned the secrets of Southeast Asian cooking while at the Raffles Hotel in Singapore. As a guest on the television show, he demonstrated this dish, in which the lively flavors of lemon grass, kaffir lime leaves, and black peppercorns spice up a light sauce for fresh lobster. Be ready to use your fingers to enjoy every tasty morsel and have plenty of rice or a baguette to soak up the sauce.

Bring a pot of water to a boil over high heat. Blanch the *choy sum* in the water for 2 minutes, or until wilted. Immediately transfer to a bowl of ice water to stop the cooking. Drain and set aside. Add the asparagus to the same pot of water and blanch for 2 to 3 minutes, until tender. Drain and immediately transfer to a bowl of ice water to stop the cooking. Drain and set aside.

Bring a very large pot of fresh water to a boil over high heat and add the salt. Plunge the lobsters into the boiling water, cover, and cook for 2 minutes, until they begin to turn red. Transfer to a bowl of ice water to stop the cooking. When cool enough to handle, break into tail, claw, and leg sections. Cut the tails into 1-inch pieces.

In a large saucepan, heat the vegetable oil over high heat to 350°F. Place the garlic in a strainer and dip into the oil for 30 to 45 seconds, until golden brown. Set aside the garlic. Measure out and set aside 1 tablespoon of the oil. Add the lobster to the oil remaining in the pan and fry for 2 to 3 minutes, until bright red and cooked through.

Place a large sauté pan over high heat. Add the reserved 1 tablespoon oil and when it is hot, add the lobster pieces. Add the lemon grass, lime leaves, chile sauce, shallot, peppercorns, and reserved garlic and toss together. Stir-fry 2 to 3 minutes to release and blend the flavors. Add the brandy and light a match to the pan to burn off the alcohol. Once the flame subsides, add the stock and soy sauce, mix well, and bring to a boil. Season with fish sauce to taste.

In a small bowl, combine the cornstarch and water and mix well. Add to the pan and stir to thicken the sauce. Add the lemon juice, green onions, and cilantro and mix well.

Divide the *choy sum* and asparagus among 4 plates. Place the lobster pieces over the vegetables along with the sauce. Serve immediately.

Desserts

Lilikoi Pudding Cake

SERVES 8

1/2 cup unsalted butter

1 1/2 cups sugar

6 eggs, separated

1/2 cup plus 2 tablespoons passion fruit purée

1/2 cup plus 2 tablespoons all-purpose flour

1 cup heavy cream

2 cups milk

1/2 teaspoon salt

Diced fresh fruit, for garnish

Lilikoi is the Hawaiian name for passion fruit, a yellow- or purple-skinned tropical fruit with lots of black seeds encased in sweet-tart, golden orange pulp. It's a luscious fruit that has its own distinctive flavor and it can be used in many preparations. This pudding cake is one—light and rich at the same time.

In a bowl, combine the butter and sugar. With an electric mixer on high speed, beat for 4 to 5 minutes, until smooth and pale. Add the egg yolks, 1 at a time, beating well after each addition. Add the purée and mix well. Add the flour and mix well. Slowly mix in the cream and milk; it's normal for the batter to look broken.

In a clean mixing bowl, beat the eggs whites and the salt with an electric mixer on high speed. Beat for 4 to 5 minutes, until soft peaks form. With a spatula, fold the whites into the batter, incorporating well. The batter will seem runny.

Lightly grease 8 (8-ounce) ramekins. Pour the batter into the ramekins and place in a baking dish. Place the baking dish in the oven and pour in hot water to come halfway up the sides of the ramekins. Bake for 35 to 40 minutes, until golden brown on top.

Remove from the oven and immediately run a knife around the edge of each ramekin. Invert each cake onto a dessert plate. Garnish with fresh fruit and serve immediately.

Roy's Tips

Ripe passion fruits feel heavy in your hand and are wrinkled on the outside. To make fresh passion fruit purée, cut the fruit open and scoop the pulp into a fine-meshed strainer or cheesecloth over a bowl. Push the fruit through the strainer or cheesecloth to remove the black seeds. Prepared passion fruit purée can be found frozen or at bakery supply stores.

If the cake doesn't come out cleanly, it has cooled too long. To remedy, place in a warm oven for 30 seconds and try again.

Hawaiian Creamsicle Panna Cotta and Brown Sugar-Caramel Sauce

SERVES 8

PANNA COTTA

5 leaves of gelatin

3¹/₂ cups heavy cream

³/₄ cup whole milk

¹/₂ cup raw white sugar

1 vanilla bean, split lengthwise and seeds scraped

Zest of 1 Kau or Valencia orange, in strips (see page 19)

1 (3- to 4-inch) cinnamon stick

SAUCE

2 tablespoons salted butter

¹/₂ cup firmly packed brown sugar

5 tablespoons heavy cream

2 teaspoons orange liqueur such as Grand Marnier, Cointreau, or orange curaçao

1 whole Kau orange, cut into sections, for garnish (see page 19)

Berries such as strawberries, blackberries, or blueberries, for garnish

Mint leaves, for garnish

Panna cotta is simply sweetened cream firmed with gelatin. Pastry chef Mark Okumura of Alan Wong's Restaurant, a guest on Hawaii Cooks with Roy Yamaguchi, *created this panna cotta as a whimsical nod to orange-flavored creamsicles. He uses Maui plantation raw white sugar, Hawaiian vanilla beans, and Kau oranges from the Big Island in this creamy yet light dessert. The caramel sauce makes it even more appealing.*

To prepare the panna cotta, place the gelatin in a bowl of cold water to soften.

In a saucepan, combine the cream, milk, sugar, vanilla bean and seeds, orange zest, and cinnamon stick. Place the pan over medium-high heat and bring to a boil. Turn off the heat and let steep for 10 minutes. Add the softened gelatin and stir to dissolve. Pour the mixture through a fine-meshed sieve and into a bowl. Place the bowl in a larger bowl filled with ice water to cool.

Lightly spray 8 (5-ounce) ramekins, custard cups, or molds with oil. When the cream mixture is cool, divide among the ramekins. Cover and refrigerate for 4 hours, or until set.

To prepare the sauce, melt the butter in a small saucepan over medium-high heat. Add the sugar, stir, and bring to a boil. Add the cream, stir, and bring to a boil. Add the liqueur and stir. Remove the pan from the heat and allow to cool.

To serve, carefully run a knife around the edges of each ramekin. Invert each onto a dessert plate. Drizzle with the sauce and decorate the plate with orange sections, berries, and mint.

Roy's Tips

If you can't find gelatin leaves, use 2¹/₂ envelopes of granular gelatin softened in ¹/₂ cup water.

Granulated sugar is a good substitute for plantation raw white sugar.

Use a vegetable peeler to remove the orange zest in strips.

The caramel sauce can be made ahead and stored in a covered container in the refrigerator. Bring it to room temperature to serve or reheat in a microwave oven. The sauce is excellent over vanilla ice cream.

Macadamia Nut Tart with Sugar Crust

SERVES 6

SUGAR CRUST

$^1/_4$ cup unsalted butter

$^2/_3$ cup sugar

2 eggs

1 teaspoon pure vanilla extract

Pinch of salt

2 cups flour

$1^1/_2$ cups unsalted macadamia nut halves or quarters

2 eggs, beaten

$^1/_2$ cup firmly packed brown sugar

$^1/_2$ cup corn syrup

$^1/_4$ cup unsalted butter

1 teaspoon pure vanilla extract

Vanilla ice cream, for garnish

Caramel sauce, for garnish

Macadamia nuts are another one of Hawaii's premier crops, crunchy and buttery rich. They are grown mostly on the island of Hawaii, where the beautiful evergreen trees cover thousands of acres. This tart, served warm with ice cream and caramel sauce, is a fine way to show off the delicate flavor of the macadamia.

To prepare the crust, in a bowl, cream together the butter and sugar. Add the eggs, vanilla, and salt and blend well. Add the flour and mix until a dough forms. Shape the dough into a round flat disc, wrap in plastic, and chill for 1 hour, or until firm.

Preheat the oven to 350°F.

On a lightly floured surface, roll out the dough to an 11-inch round, $^1/_4$ inch thick. Transfer the dough to a 9-inch removable-bottom tart pan and press into the bottom and sides of the pan. Trim the edges and discard the excess dough. Line the pastry shell with aluminum foil and fill with pie weights or beans. Bake for 10 to 12 minutes, until light golden brown. Remove from the oven and place on a rack to cool slightly.

Decrease the oven to 325°F. Fill the bottom of the pastry shell with the nuts, spreading evenly.

Place the eggs in a bowl. In a small saucepan, combine the sugar, syrup, butter, and vanilla over medium-high heat. When the mixture begins to bubble around the edges, remove from the heat. Slowly add about one-third of the sugar mixture to the eggs, whisking constantly. Pour the egg mixture back into the sugar mixture and blend well. Pour through a fine-meshed sieve over the nuts. Place in the oven and bake for 15 to 20 minutes, until golden brown. Remove from the oven and allow to cool on a rack. Serve warm, garnished with ice cream and caramel sauce.

Roy's Tip

Macadamia nuts tend to shard when they are chopped. To avoid this, cut whole nuts in quarters or halves, one by one.

Chocolate Mousse

SERVES 8

4 ounces Hawaiian Chocolate Factory
  dark chocolate or other semisweet
  chocolate (see page 19)

5 eggs, separated

3 tablespoons sugar

Strawberries, quartered, for garnish

Bananas, sliced, for garnish

Brothers Philippe and Pierre Padovani of Padovani's Restaurant are known for their delicious chocolate confections, one of which they showcased when they appeared on the show with me. In their experiments with Hawaiian-grown and processed chocolate from the island of Hawaii, they created this light, airy chocolate mousse.

Break or chop the chocolate into small pieces and place in the top of a double boiler set over barely simmering water. Stir constantly until melted. Remove from the heat and allow to cool slightly.

Place the egg yolks in a bowl and beat well with a whisk. Add 1 tablespoon of the sugar and continue to beat for 3 to 5 minutes, until very fluffy. Add the chocolate to the egg yolks and mix well with a spatula.

Place the egg whites in a large bowl and beat with a whisk. Slowly add the remaining 2 tablespoons sugar and beat until the egg whites are stiff but not dry.

Scoop one-fourth of the egg whites into the chocolate and fold in with a spatula. Gently and quickly fold in the remaining egg whites. Pour the mixture into 8 (5-ounce) ramekins or dessert bowls. Cover and refrigerate for at least 4 hours, or until set.

To serve, decorate each ramekin with strawberries and bananas. Serve immediately.

Roy's Tips

This chocolate mousse is best when eaten the same day it is prepared.

This recipe contains raw eggs, which should be avoided by pregnant women, the elderly, and people with compromised immune systems.

Coconut Panna Cotta

SERVES 6

2 envelopes granular gelatin

6 tablespoons water

2 cups coconut milk

$1^1/_4$ cups heavy cream

$^3/_4$ cup sugar

1 teaspoon pure vanilla extract

Fresh diced fruit, for garnish

Coconut is used in both savory and sweet preparations in the cooking of Southeast Asia and the Pacific. Its flavor is distinctive and its richness even more pronounced in this creamy version of panna cotta.

In a small bowl, combine the gelatin with the water until softened.

In a saucepan, combine the coconut milk, cream, sugar, and vanilla. Place over medium heat and warm until hot to the touch (about 110°F). Add the gelatin and stir until dissolved. Pour into 6 (5-ounce) ramekins or custard cups. Cover and refrigerate for 4 hours, or until set.

Serve garnished with fresh fruit.

Minted Mango Martini Float with Crystallized Ginger

SERVES 6

MANGO SORBET

2 cups water

2 ripe mangoes, peeled, seeded, and sliced

$^1/_2$ cup sugar

2 tablespoons freshly squeezed lemon juice

SYRUP

1 cup water

1 cup sugar

1 stalk lemon grass, cut into $^1/_2$-inch slices

3 tablespoons whole black peppercorns

5 sprigs mint

Raw sugar, for dipping

2 ripe mangoes, peeled, seeded, and sliced

$^1/_4$ cup crystallized ginger, cut into strips, for garnish

Julienned fresh mint, for garnish

Lemon grass sticks, for garnish

A refreshingly light mango martini is a fine way to enjoy the summer mango season in Hawaii. Chef Ronnie Nasuti of Roy's Restaurant appeared on the show to demonstrate this delightful combination of fresh mango and mango sorbet, capturing the wonderful essence of ripe mangoes. Crystallized ginger adds a lively dimension to the Asian-themed flavors.

To prepare the mango sorbet, combine the water, mangoes, sugar, and lemon juice in a blender and purée until smooth. Pour the mixture into an ice cream maker and freeze according to the manufacturer's directions. Place the sorbet in the freezer until ready to serve. Cover and store the remaining mangoes in the refrigerator.

To prepare the syrup, combine the water, sugar, lemon grass, peppercorns, and mint in a saucepan and bring to a boil over high heat. Boil for 1 minute to dissolve the sugar. Turn off the heat and let steep until cool. Pour through a fine-meshed strainer, place in a covered container, and refrigerate until cold.

To serve, moisten the rim of 6 martini glasses with water and dip in the raw sugar. Divide the sorbet among the glasses and top with the sliced mangoes. Pour the syrup over, and garnish with ginger, mint, and lemon grass sticks. Serve immediately.

Roy's Tips

The sorbet can be made several days ahead and stored in a covered container in the freezer. The syrup can be made ahead too, and stored in the refrigerator.

To make the assembly of this dessert easy and quick, scoop the sorbet ahead of time and place in a covered shallow dish in the freezer. Have all the garnishes ready to fill the martini glasses at serving time.

White Pirie Mango Tart

SERVES 6

LEMON CONFIT
1 large lemon

$1/4$ cup kosher salt

$3/4$ cup sugar

$1/2$ cup water

MANGO TART
1 recipe sugar crust dough (page 141)

6 cups diced White Pirie or other fresh mango (see page 18)

$1/4$ cup sugar

1 teaspoon pure vanilla extract

2 tablespoons cornstarch

$1/2$ teaspoon freshly grated nutmeg

1 teaspoon freshly grated ginger

2 tablespoons freshly squeezed lemon juice

$3/4$ cup flour

$3/4$ cup instant oatmeal

$3/4$ cup finely chopped macadamia nuts

$3/4$ cup firmly packed light brown sugar

$3/4$ cup unsalted butter, chilled and diced

Vanilla ice cream, for serving

Blueberries, for garnish

When Island-born chef Kelvin Ro appeared on Hawaii Cooks *with Roy Yamaguchi, he featured the White Pirie mango—an aromatic, lusciously sweet fruit prized among mango aficionados. This mango tart is a treat, especially with the lemony accent that sets the taste buds up for all the sweetness that lies within the fruit.*

To prepare the lemon confit, slice the lemon into thin rings and remove and discard the pulp. Combine the lemon rind, salt, and $1/4$ cup of the sugar in a small bowl and marinate at room temperature overnight.

Rinse the lemon rind well to remove the salt and sugar. Combine the remaining $1/2$ cup sugar and the water in a small saucepan and bring to a boil over high heat. Boil for 1 minute. Decrease the heat to low and add the lemon rind. Simmer for 30 to 45 minutes, until the rind is soft but not brown. Remove the rind from the syrup and allow to cool. Discard the syrup. Cover and refrigerate until ready to use.

To prepare the tart, preheat the oven to 350°F and place a rack in the center position.

On a lightly floured surface, roll out the dough to a 12-inch round, a little less than $1/4$ inch thick. Transfer the dough to a 9-inch pie pan and press into the bottom and sides of the pan. Trim the edges and discard the excess dough.

In a large bowl, combine the mango, sugar, vanilla, cornstarch, nutmeg, ginger, lemon juice, and lemon confit. Gently mix the ingredients together.

Place the flour, oatmeal, macadamia nuts, sugar, and butter in another bowl. Using a pastry blender, combine the ingredients, incorporating the butter until it forms pea-sized pieces.

Fill the pastry shell with the mango mixture and top with the flour mixture. Bake for 45 to 50 minutes, until the topping is golden brown. Remove from the oven and allow to cool on a rack. Serve warm, with ice cream and blueberries.

Roy's Tip
You can also prepare this as a mango crisp without the bottom crust.

Hot Chocolate Soufflé

SERVES 8

1 cup sugar

1/3 cup firmly packed brown sugar

6 tablespoons cornstarch

3/4 cup unsalted butter

8 ounces semisweet chocolate, cut into small pieces

2 eggs

2 egg yolks

This is one of Roy's Restaurants' classic desserts, a rich soufflé dense with chocolate. Use the best chocolate you can find and this delicious dessert will taste even better. The soufflé can be prepared a day ahead and baked just before serving. Be sure to set a timer; the baking time is exact. You can't go wrong with whipped cream or vanilla ice cream as an accompaniment.

In a bowl, combine the sugar, brown sugar, and cornstarch and mix well.

In a saucepan, melt the butter over medium-high heat. When the butter is bubbling, add the chocolate and stir with a spoon until the chocolate is melted and the mixture is smooth. When bubbles begin to form at the edges, remove from the heat.

Add the chocolate to the sugar mixture and stir well. Add the eggs and egg yolks, 1 at a time, mixing well after each addition. Pour through a fine-meshed sieve into a bowl. Cover and refrigerate for 4 to 6 hours or up to overnight, until thick.

Preheat the oven to 375°F.

Place 8 (3-inch) metal rings on a baking sheet lined with parchment paper. Line each ring with a 2-inch strip of greased parchment paper. Or, lightly grease 8 (5-ounce) ramekins or custard cups.

Scoop the mixture into the rings, about two-thirds full. Bake for 20 minutes. The soufflé should be crisped on the outside but runny on the inside. Remove from the oven. Slide a spatula under each ring, lift, and transfer to a dessert plate. Gently lift off the ring and remove the parchment paper. Serve immediately.

Basics

Chicken Stock

MAKES ABOUT 1 QUART

1 to 2 chicken carcasses, separated into pieces

2 tablespoons olive oil

1 celery stalk, coarsely chopped

$^1/_2$ cup coarsely chopped onion

$^1/_3$ cup coarsely chopped carrot

4 quarts water

$^1/_4$ cup loosely packed fresh sweet basil leaves

2 tablespoons fresh thyme leaves

5 black peppercorns

2 bay leaves

Salt and freshly ground black pepper

Preheat the oven to 350°F.

Place the chicken bones in a roasting pan and sprinkle with $1^1/_2$ tablespoons of the oil. Roast for 15 to 20 minutes, until brown.

Heat the remaining $^1/_2$ tablespoon olive oil in a large stockpot over medium-high heat. Add the celery, onion, and carrot and sauté for 5 to 7 minutes, until tender. Add the water, basil, thyme, peppercorns, bay leaves, and roasted bones. Bring to a boil, skimming the surface of the stock to remove any impurities. Decrease the heat to medium and simmer for 45 minutes, or until reduced by three-quarters.

Pass through a fine-meshed sieve, discarding the solids. Allow to cool and then refrigerate. Skim the surface to remove any fat. Reheat to use, and season with salt and pepper. Store, covered, in the refrigerator for up to 2 days or in the freezer for up to 6 months.

Toasted Coconut Flakes

Preheat the oven to 325°F. Spread flaked coconut on a baking sheet. Place in the oven and toast for 10 to 15 minutes, until golden brown. Remove from the oven and allow to cool.

Sautéed Garlic and Garlic Oil

MAKES ABOUT 1¹/₂ TABLESPOONS SAUTÉED GARLIC AND ¹/₄ CUP GARLIC OIL

¹/₄ cup vegetable oil
2 tablespoons minced fresh garlic

Place a small sauté pan over medium heat. Add the oil and when it is hot, add the garlic. Cook for about 2 minutes, stirring every 30 seconds, until the garlic just begins to turn color. Remove the pan from the heat and let the mixture steep until it is cool. Drain to use as sautéed garlic; strain to use as garlic oil. Store, covered, in the refrigerator for up to 3 days.

Sautéed Ginger and Ginger Oil

MAKES ABOUT 1¹/₂ TABLESPOONS SAUTÉED GINGER AND ¹/₄ CUP GINGER OIL

¹/₄ cup vegetable oil
2 tablespoons minced fresh ginger

Place a small sauté pan over medium heat. Add the oil and when it is hot, add the ginger. Cook for 1¹/₂ to 2 minutes, stirring every 30 seconds, until the ginger just begins to turn golden brown. Remove the pan from the heat and let the mixture steep until it is cool. Drain to use as sautéed ginger; strain to use as ginger oil. Store, covered, in the refrigerator for up to 3 days.

Mangoes

To get the most flesh out of a mango, take a look at its somewhat flat oval shape. The pit or seed is flat, running vertically from stem to pointed end. Make two cuts on either side of the flat seed, then trim the other two narrow portions. Cut away the skin then cut the mango into slices, julienne strips, chunks, or a dice.

Mung Bean Noodles

To prevent scattering, place the noodles in a large paper bag and break to separate them. One and a half ounces of dry noodles will yield about 1 cup of cooked noodles.

Bring a quart of water to a boil over high heat and add the noodles. Cook for about 3 minutes, or until tender. Drain and rinse under cool water.

Caramelized Pineapple

MAKES 1 POUND

1 (3- to 4-pound) fresh pineapple
1 cup water
1/2 cup sugar

Break off the crown of the pineapple. Cut off 1 inch of the top and bottom and stand upright on a cutting board. Trim from top to bottom, removing about 1/2 inch of the rind and the eyes imbedded in the flesh. Cut the pineapple crosswise into 1/2-inch slices and cut each slice into 4 wedges.

Preheat the oven to 250°F.

Combine the water and sugar in a small saucepan over medium-high heat. Bring to a boil and continue to boil for 1 minute to dissolve the sugar. Remove from the heat.

Line a baking sheet with parchment paper. Dip the pineapple wedges into the sugar syrup and transfer to the baking sheet. Bake for 2 1/2 hours, or until the pineapple has dried and the sugar is golden brown. Remove from the oven and allow to cool. Store in a cool place in an airtight container for up to 1 month.

Toasted Rice Powder

Heat raw white rice in a small sauté pan over medium-high heat. Toast for 3 to 4 minutes, shaking the pan occasionally, until golden brown. Remove from the heat and allow to cool. Transfer the rice to a spice grinder and grind to a powder. Store in an airtight container.

Toasted Sesame Seeds

Heat white sesame seeds in a small sauté pan over medium-high heat. Toast for 2 to 3 minutes, shaking the pan occasionally, until golden brown and the seeds start popping. Remove from the heat and transfer to a dish to cool. For ground sesame seeds, transfer to a mortar and pestle and crush. Toasted seeds should be used within a few days.

Sautéed Shallots and Shallot Oil

MAKES ABOUT 1¹/₂ TABLESPOONS SAUTÉED SHALLOT AND ¹/₄ CUP SHALLOT OIL

¹/₄ cup vegetable oil

2 tablespoons minced shallot, about 1 whole shallot

Place a small sauté pan over medium heat. Add the oil and when it is hot, add the shallots. Cook for 3 to 4 minutes, stirring every 30 seconds, until the shallot just begins to turn light golden brown. Remove the pan from the heat and let the mixture steep until it is cool. Drain to use as sautéed shallot; strain to use as shallot oil. Store, covered, in the refrigerator for up to 3 days.

Shrimp Stock

MAKES ABOUT 2 QUARTS

2 pounds shrimp shells
1 carrot, sliced
1 celery stalk, sliced
1 small onion, sliced
3 cloves garlic
1 teaspoon chopped fresh thyme
1 bunch fresh parsley, tied
6 black peppercorns
2 bay leaves
3 quarts water
Salt and freshly ground black pepper

Preheat the oven to 350°F.

Spread the shrimp shells in a roasting pan and roast for 15 to 20 minutes, until dried. Place the shells in a stockpot along with the carrot, celery, onion, garlic, thyme, parsley, peppercorns, bay leaves, and water. Bring to a boil over high heat, skimming the surface to remove any impurities. Decrease the heat to low and simmer for 1 hour, or until the liquid has been reduced by one-third. Pass through a fine-meshed sieve, discarding the solids, and season with salt and pepper to taste. Store, covered, in the refrigerator for up to 2 days or in the freezer for up to 2 months.

FOR FISH STOCK: Substitute 2 pounds of bones or scraps from lean, white fish for the shrimp shells. Rinse the bones and scraps under cold running water but do not roast.

Teriyaki Sauce

MAKES ABOUT 1 CUP

1 cup soy sauce
1 tablespoon minced garlic
1 tablespoon minced ginger
1 cup sugar

Combine all the ingredients in a saucepan and bring to a boil over medium-high heat. Decrease the heat to low and simmer, stirring occasionally, for about 15 minutes, until the mixture is syrupy and reduced by one-third. Store in a covered jar in the refrigerator for up to 2 weeks.

Tomatoes

To peel a tomato, bring a saucepan of water to a boil over high heat. With the tip of a knife, remove the core of the tomato. Cut an X in the opposite end. Place the tomato in a slotted spoon and lower into the boiling water. Blanch for 10 seconds. Remove with the spoon and immediately plunge into a bowl of ice water to stop the cooking. When the tomato is cool enough to handle, slip off the skin.

To seed a tomato, cut it in half crosswise. Squeeze each half to extract the seeds.

To make fresh tomato juice, peel fresh, ripe tomatoes. Seed the tomatoes over a fine-meshed sieve, capturing the juices. Purée the flesh in a blender, adding the juices, until very smooth.

Basic Tomato Sauce

MAKES ABOUT 2 CUPS

1 tablespoon extra virgin olive oil

1 tablespoon minced fresh garlic

6 fresh ripe tomatoes, coarsely chopped, or 1 (28-ounce) can whole tomatoes

2 tablespoons minced fresh basil

Place a saucepan over medium-high heat. Add the olive oil and when it is hot, add the garlic and sauté for 20 to 30 seconds, until barely light golden brown. Add the tomatoes, and cook until bubbling. Decrease the heat to medium-low and simmer, uncovered, for about 30 minutes, or until the sauce is thick. Remove from the heat and allow to cool.

Transfer the sauce to a food processor and purée until smooth. Return to the saucepan and continue to cook for 5 to 10 minutes, until the liquid has evaporated and the sauce is very thick. Add the basil and simmer for another 5 minutes.

Use with pasta or as an ingredient in other preparations. Store, covered, in the refrigerator for 2 to 3 days or in the freezer for up to 3 months.

Taro Leaves

Taro leaves must be well cooked to neutralize the calcium oxalate crystals that can cause itchiness in the mouth and throat. To cook, place 1 pound of leaves in a covered saucepan with 1 cup of water. Place the pan over high heat and as soon as the water is steaming, decrease the heat to low. Cook for 30 minutes, or until the leaves are soft and tender. Allow to cool, then squeeze out the excess water. A pound of uncooked taro leaves will yield about 1 cup of cooked, well-drained leaves.

Veal Stock and Demi-Glace

MAKES ABOUT 2 QUARTS STOCK

1 to 2 pounds veal bones

1/4 cup coarsely chopped celery

1/4 cup coarsely chopped carrot

1/2 cup coarsely chopped onion

1/2 cup coarsely chopped tomatoes

2 tablespoons coarsely chopped mushroom stems

2 cloves garlic

1 tablespoon tomato purée

1/2 cup loosely packed fresh sweet basil leaves

1/2 teaspoon minced fresh thyme

1 bay leaf, julienned

3 black peppercorns

6 quarts water

Salt and freshly ground black pepper

Preheat the oven to 350°F. Place the bones, celery, carrot, onion, tomatoes, mushroom stems, garlic, tomato purée, basil, thyme, bay leaf, and peppercorns in a roasting pan. Toss together and roast for 20 to 30 minutes, until the bones are dark brown.

Transfer the contents of the roasting pan to a stockpot, add the water, and bring to a boil over high heat. Skim the surface of the stock to remove any impurities. Decrease the heat to medium and simmer for about 2 hours, or until reduced by half. Pass through a fine-meshed sieve, discarding the solids. Allow to cool and then refrigerate. Skim the surface to remove any fat. Reheat to use, and season with salt and pepper. Store, covered, in the refrigerator for up to 2 days or in the freezer for up to 6 months.

To prepare demi-glace, bring the unseasoned veal stock to a boil over high heat. Decrease the heat to medium and simmer for about 1 hour, until dark and syrupy and reduced by three-quarters.

For a fortified stock and demi-glace, add a pound of beef bones, preferably with some meat on them, to the stock.

Acknowledgments

A heartfelt thank you to all who helped put this project together. We greatly appreciate all who contributed so generously of their time and resources.

Putting together a book is not an easy endeavor and we are deeply grateful to the cowriter of this book, Joan Namkoong, and the editor, Holly Taines White, for their patience and commitment. We also owe a huge debt of gratitude to Eleanor Nakama-Mitsunaga and Debra Kee-Chong, who have put in countless hours of hard work on both this book and the television series; your dedication and loyalty mean so much!

To Roy's restaurant staff, who make things so easy, even in the most challenging situations, we send a very big *mahalo* to all of you, and we would especially like to thank Mona Moore, Robbyn Shim, Jacqueline Lau, Ronnie Nasuti, Noah French, and Rainer Kumbroch.

Hawaii Cooks with Roy Yamaguchi, the television series, is now more than a decade old, and this book is a celebration and testament to all who have supported us. Many thanks to Senator Carol Fukunaga; Mike McCartney and the staff of PBS Hawaii; series' director, Robert Bates; our wine team, Chuck Furuya and Robert Kowal; Joy Chong-Stannard; and our generous sponsors over the years, Mauna Loa Macadamia Nut Corporation, the Hawaii Visitors and Convention Bureau, the Hawaii State Department of Agriculture, the Department of Business Economic Development and Tourism, Sub-Zero/Wolf, Castle & Cooke, and Kikkoman International.

To Jo Ann Deck and Phil Wood of Ten Speed Press, thank you for your dedication and commitment to this project.

While there are far too many to list individually, we owe so much to our Hawaii community of chefs, food producers, and farmers. Your dedication and hard work are a continuous source of inspiration and we thank you.

—Roy Yamaguchi and Melanie Kosaka

About the Author

Roy Yamaguchi is one of Hawaii's most celebrated chefs. He was born and raised in Yokohama, Japan, but his familial roots are in Hawaii: his father was born and raised on Maui, where Roy's grandfather owned a grocery store and restaurants. Roy would help his grandfather during summer visits to Maui and at the age of nine announced that someday he would be a chef, just like his grandfather.

Upon graduating from high school at eighteen, he ventured to New York and the Culinary Institute of America (CIA) for his formal culinary training. Here, Roy was exposed to American and European ingredients he had never seen before and was trained in the classic techniques of French cuisine.

After the CIA, Roy headed to Los Angeles where he gained experience and confidence as a chef, mostly in the French tradition. It was also here that he began to tinker with mixing his French training with Asian ingredients, a fusion that evolved into his own distinct Euro-Asian style. At 385 North, the first restaurant he would call his own, he garnered rave reviews and nominations for California's Chef of the Year in 1986 and 1987. But by then his sights were set on Hawaii.

Roy's, the restaurant, opened in 1988 in an office building in the residential neighborhood of Hawaii Kai in East Honolulu—not your typical restaurant venue. But Roy capitalized on the bounty of fresh island seafood, meats, vegetables, and fruits, seasoned them with the flavors of his childhood, and cooked them with the passion of the finest of French chefs. It was an instant hit among residents and visitors alike and word traveled quickly about his innovative style of cooking. The opening of Roy's was a landmark in Hawaii's culinary history and earned him a James Beard Foundation Award in 1993.

Roy's keen sense of business, competitive spirit, and focused attention to cooking catapulted his restaurant philosophy into a growing empire of fine dining establishments throughout the state of Hawaii, the nation, and the world. At last count there were thirty-plus Roy's restaurants and it won't be long before there's a Roy's in every state, serving the finest flavors Hawaii has to offer.

For Roy, food and cooking are his life. He is a thoughtful chef who can assemble ingredients and visualize the process in which flavors and textures will produce uncompromisingly delicious food, even when it is just for a television camera. He is, above all, a master chef.

Index

A

Ahi
  about, 36
  Ahi Salad with Miso Dressing, 82
Aku
  about, 37
  Aku Tataki, 63
Alaea, 15
Anchovies, 12
Apple bananas
  about, 18
  Mahimahi with Citrus Sauce,
    Apple Bananas, and
    Macadamia Nuts, 116
Apple-Curry Sauce, 94
Artichokes, 40
Arugula, 40
Asai, Kesuke "Casey," 63
Asian-Style Spicy Peppercorn
  Steak, 92

B

Bamboo shoots, 91
Bananas. *See* Apple bananas
Barbecue Salmon, 109–10
Basil, 31
Beans. *See also* Black beans;
  Edamame
  haricots verts, 41
  Seared Scallop Salad, 85
  Shrimp Risotto, 128

Stir-Fried Vegetables, 100
Tuscan-Style Pasta with White
  Beans and Pork, 102
yard-long, 45
Béarnaise Sauce, 72
Beef, 51
  Asian-Style Spicy Peppercorn
    Steak, 92
  Grilled Chuck Steak, 90–91
  Portuguese-Style Steak
    Sandwich, 93
Bitter melon, 24
  removing bitterness from, 99
  Tofu-Yuba Stir-Fry, 98–99
Bitterness, 3, 24
Black beans
  Black Bean Sauce, 100
  fermented, 13
Bloody Mary, 74
Bok choy, 40
Broccolini, 40
  Pad Thai-Style Noodles, 90–91
  Pan-Seared Chicken with Honey
    Sauce, Couscous, and
    Vegetables, 106–7
Brown Sugar-Caramel Sauce, 140
Butter, 52

C

Cake, Lilikoi Pudding, 138
Cassoulet of Offal, 114–15

Caviar
  about, 29
  Champagne-Caviar Sauce, 67
Celery cabbage. *See* Won bok
Champagne-Caviar Sauce, 67
Char siu, 51
  Char Siu Pork Chops, 100
  Pineapple Fried Rice, 112
  Thai Black Rice Risotto, 103–4
Chervil, 31
Chicken
  MediterAsian Saffron Chicken, 111
  Pan-Seared Chicken with Honey
    Sauce, 106–7
  Salt-Crusted Chicken (variation),
    103–4
  Shichimi Chicken, 109
  Spicy Chicken Wings, 66
  Steamed Chicken Breast with
    Vegetables, 105
  stock, 150
Chile oils, 25
Chile peppers, 4, 25
Chile pepper water, 26
Chile sauces, 26
Chin, Leann, 121
Chinese cabbage. *See* Won bok
Chinese New Year, 52, 121
Chinese-Style Whole Steamed
  Fish, 118
Chives, 33

Chocolate
    Chocolate Mousse, 142
    Hawaiian, 19
    Hot Chocolate Soufflé, 147
Choy sum
    about, 40
    Stir-Fried Lobster with Spicy
      Garlic and Black Pepper
      Sauce, 134
Chuck's Lamb Chops Pupu, 73
Cilantro, 32
Cioppino, Hawaiian, 131-32
Citrus fruits, 22
Citrus Sauce, 116
Clams
    Hawaiian Cioppino, 131-32
    Shrimp and Clam Linguine, 126
Cocktails
    Bloody Mary, 74
    Pineapple Vodka, 74
Coconut flakes, toasted, 150
Coconut milk, 52-53
    Coconut Curry Sauce, 112
    Coconut Panna Cotta, 143
    Taro Sauce, 98
    Thai Black Rice Risotto, 103-4
    Thai Peanut Sauce, 117
Color, adding, 6
Corn
    Hawaiian Cioppino, 131-32
    Pad Thai-Style Noodles, 90-91
    removing canned flavor
      from, 91
    sprouts, 41, 42
Couscous, Pan-Seared Chicken with,
    106-7
Crab
    Crab and Taro Cakes, 72
    Crab with Vanilla Sauce, 129
    eggs, 29
    Hawaiian Cioppino, 131-32
    Kona, 37

    Molded Sushi with Unagi and
      Spicy Crab, 71
    steaming and cleaning, 132
Cream, 53
Crostini, 131
Cured Salmon and Tomato Salad, 83
Curry pastes, 14-15, 27
Curry powders, 27

D

Daikon, 41
Dashi, 55
Demi-glace, 54, 156
Dipping Sauce, 66
Duck Salad, Roasted, 7-8, 78-79
Dumplings, Seafood Full Moon, 68-69

E

Eastern Rouille, 131
Edamame, 41
    preparing, 62
    Wok-Charred Edamame, 62
Eggs
    Crab and Taro Cakes, 72
    Hot Chocolate Soufflé, 147
    raw, 142

F

Fish
    Ahi Salad with Miso Dressing, 82
    Aku Tataki, 63
    Barbecue Salmon, 109-10
    Chinese-Style Whole Steamed
      Fish, 118
    Cured Salmon and Tomato
      Salad, 83
    Hawaiian Cioppino, 131-32
    Lemon Grass-Crusted Hawaiian
      Shutome, 117
    Mahimahi with Citrus Sauce,
      Apple Bananas, and
      Macadamia Nuts, 116

    Ponape Pepper-Crusted Shutome,
      114-15
    Seafood Full Moon Dumplings
      with Crispy Ogo, 68-69
    Steamed Opakapaka and
      Salmon with Shrimp Mousse,
      120
    Thai-Style Deep-Fried Mullet,
      112-13
    varieties of, 36-38
Fish sauce, 13
Flavor components, 2-3, 11, 12. *See
    also individual flavors*
Foo jook, 99
Fresh Pasta with Shrimp, Pancetta,
    Anchovy, and Garlic, 122-23
Fruits, 18-19. *See also individual
    fruits*
    citrus, 22
    Fruit Vinaigrette, 85
Furikake, 30
Furuya, Chuck, 73

G

Galangal, 34
Game Hen, Salt-Crusted Cornish,
    103-4
Gari, 22, 33
Garlic, 32-33
    oil, 151
    sautéed, 151
    Spicy Garlic and Black Pepper
      Sauce, 134
    stir-frying, 62
Gelatin, 140
Ginger, 31, 33-34
    juice, pickled, 22
    juice, pure, 34
    oil, 151
    pickled, 22, 33
    sautéed, 151
    stir-frying, 62

Glazes
  Honey Glaze, 97
  Miso Glaze, 98
Golden Shrimp-Stuffed Tofu, 121
Green Growers Farm, 44
Greens, 24. *See also individual*
  varieties
  micro-, 42
  Warm Tofu Salad of Wilted
    Greens, 80
Grilled Chuck Steak, 90–91
Gyoza wrappers, 47

H

Haricots verts, 41
Hawaiian Cioppino, 131–32
Hawaiian Creamsicle Panna
  Cotta, 140
Hawaiian Plate Lunch, 109–10
Herbs and spices, 31–35
Hirabayashi, Wayne, 134
Hoisin, 13
Honey, 19
  Honey Glaze, 97
  Honey Sauce, 106
Hot Chocolate Soufflé, 147

I, J

Ikura, 29
Iwamoto Natto and Noodle
  Factory, 48
Jam, Pineapple-Mango, 64

K

Kabayaki, 17
Kaiware, 41, 42
Kalua Pork with Taro Sauce, 98–99
Kau oranges, 19
Ko chu jang, 26
Kona cold lobster, 37
  Kona Cold Lobster with Spicy
    Mango Sauce, 133

Stir-Fried Lobster with Spicy
  Garlic and Black Pepper
  Sauce, 134
Konbu, 30

L

Lamb, 51
  Chuck's Lamb Chops Pupu, 73
  Lamb Steaks with Okinawan
    Sweet Potato Mash, 94
  Mediterranean-Style Lamb with
    Crispy Ginger, 96
Lemon Confit, 146
Lemon grass, 31, 35
Lemon Grass-Crusted Hawaiian
  Shutome, 117
Lilikoi Pudding Cake, 138
Lime leaves, kaffir, 31, 35
Lobster. *See Kona cold lobster*
Lumpia wrappers, 47
Lychee, 18

M

Macadamia nuts, 53
  chopping, 141
  Macadamia Nut Tart, 141
  oil, 53
Macaroni Salad, 109
Mahimahi
  about, 38
  Mahimahi with Citrus Sauce,
    Apple Bananas, and
    Macadamia Nuts, 116
Mangoes, 18
  Mango Sauce, 103
  Mango Sorbet, 144
  Minted Mango Martini Float, 144
  Pickled Mango Vinaigrette, 86
  Pineapple-Mango Jam, 64
  preparing, 151
  Roasted Duck Salad with Deep-
    Fried Tofu and Mango, 7–8, 78–79

Seared Scallop Salad with
  Mangoes, 85
Spicy Mango Sauce, 133
Thai Black Rice Risotto, 103–4
White Pirie Mango Tart, 146
Marinade, Pineapple, 97
Masago, 29
MediterAsian Saffron Chicken, 111
Mediterranean-Style Lamb, 96
Mempachi
  about, 38
  Hawaiian Cioppino, 131–32
Meneji, 33
Mentaiko, 29
Mesclun, 42
Micro-greens, 42
Minted Mango Martini Float, 144
Mirin, 19
Miso, 14
  Miso Dressing, 82
  Miso Glaze, 98
Mitsuba, 31
Mizuna, 42
Molded Sushi with Unagi and Spicy
  Crab, 71
Mousse
  Chocolate Mousse, 142
  Shrimp Mousse, 120
MSG, 3
Mullet
  about, 38
  Thai-Style Deep-Fried Mullet,
    112–13
Mung bean noodles, 47
  cooking, 152
  Shrimp and Scallop Spring
    Rolls, 67
  Warm Tofu Salad of Wilted
    Greens, 80
Mushrooms, 42–43
Mustard greens, 43
Myoga, 34

N

Nalo Farms, 43
Napa cabbage. *See* Won bok
Nasuti, Ronnie, 144
Noodles, 47-48. *See also* Mung bean
     noodles; Pasta
     factory, 48
     Pad Thai-Style Noodles, 90-91
     Vietnamese-Style Cold Udon with
          Shrimp, 124
Nori, 30

O

Oceany flavor, 12, 29-30
Offal, Cassoulet of, 114-15
Ogawa, Faith, 82
Ogo
     about, 30
     Seafood Full Moon Dumplings
          with Crispy Ogo, 68-69
Okimoto, Dean, 43
Okumura, Mark, 140
Olive oil, 83
Onions
     green, 32-33
     Maui, 41, 63
Opakapaka, 38
     Seafood Full Moon Dumplings,
          68-69
     Steamed Opakapaka and Salmon
          with Shrimp Mousse, 120
Oranges
     Citrus Sauce, 116
     Kau, 19
Oyster sauce, 14

P

Padovani, Philippe and Pierre, 142
Palm sugar, 20
Pancetta, 51
     Fresh Pasta with Shrimp, Pancetta,
          Anchovy, and Garlic, 122-23

Steamed Opakapaka and Salmon
     with Shrimp Mousse, 120
Tuscan-Style Pasta with White
     Beans and Pork, 102
Panko, 48
Panna cotta
     Coconut Panna Cotta, 143
     Hawaiian Creamsicle Panna
          Cotta, 140
Pan-Seared Chicken with Honey
Sauce, 106-7
Passion fruit, 18
     Lilikoi Pudding Cake, 138
     purée, 138
     syrup, 116
Pasta. *See also* Noodles
     cooking, 123
     Fresh Pasta with Shrimp, Pancetta,
          Anchovy, and Garlic, 122-23
     Macaroni Salad, 109
     Shrimp and Clam Linguine, 126
     Tuscan-Style Pasta, 102
Peanut Sauce, Thai, 117
Peas
     snap, 44
     sprouts, 42
Peppercorns, 27, 115
Perilla. *See Shiso*
Pineapples, 18
     caramelized, 152
     Pineapple Fried Rice, 112
     Pineapple-Mango Jam, 64
     Pineapple Marinade, 97
     Pineapple Rice, 109-10
     Pineapple Vodka, 74
     Roast Pork with Caramelized
          Pineapple, 97
Plate Lunch, Hawaiian, 109-10
Poi, 48-49
Poke, 36, 37
Ponape Pepper-Crusted Shutome,
     114-15

Ponzu, 17
Pork. *See also Char siu;* Pancetta;
     Sausage
     Cassoulet of Offal, 114-15
     Char Siu Pork Chops with Black
          Bean Sauce, 100
     Kalua Pork with Taro Sauce,
          98-99
     Roast Pork with Caramelized
          Pineapple, 97
     Tuscan-Style Pasta with White
          Beans and Pork, 102
Portuguese-Style Steak Sandwich, 93

R

Radicchio, 43
Rasmussen, Ruth, 62
Rayu, 25
Rice
     cooking, 49
     Molded Sushi with Unagi and
          Spicy Crab, 71
     Pineapple Fried Rice, 112
     Pineapple Rice, 109-10
     powder, toasted, 153
     Shrimp Risotto, 128
     Thai Black Rice Risotto, 103-4
     varieties of, 49-50
     washing, 49
Ro, Kelvin, 146
Roasted Duck Salad, 7-8, 78-79
Roast Pork with Caramelized
Pineapple, 97
Rouille, Eastern, 131

S

Saimin
     about, 48
     Pad Thai-Style Noodles, 90-91
Sake
     about, 19-20
     Sake-Soy Sauce, 63

Salad dressings
    Fruit Vinaigrette, 85
    Miso Dressing, 82
    Pickled Mango Vinaigrette, 86
    Soy Vinaigrette, 105
Salads
    Ahi Salad with Miso Dressing, 82
    Cured Salmon and Tomato
      Salad, 83
    Macaroni Salad, 109
    Roasted Duck Salad, 7-8, 78-79
    Seared Scallop Salad with
      Mangoes, 85
    Warm Tofu Salad of Wilted
      Greens, 80
Salmon
    Barbecue Salmon, 109-10
    Cured Salmon and Tomato
      Salad, 83
    Steamed Opakapaka and Salmon
      with Shrimp Mousse, 120
Salt, 15, 17
Salt-Crusted Cornish Game Hen,
    103-4
Saltiness, 2, 12-17
Sambal oelek, 26
Sandwich, Portuguese-Style
    Steak, 93
Sauces
    Apple-Curry Sauce, 94
    Béarnaise Sauce, 72
    Black Bean Sauce, 100
    Brown Sugar-Caramel Sauce, 140
    Champagne-Caviar Sauce, 67
    chile, 26
    Citrus Sauce, 116
    Coconut Curry Sauce, 112
    Dipping Sauce, 66
    fish, 13
    hoisin, 13
    Honey Sauce, 106
    kabayaki, 17

Mango Sauce, 103
oyster, 14
Sake-Soy Sauce, 63
soy, 16-17
Spicy Garlic and Black Pepper
    Sauce, 134
Spicy Mango Sauce, 133
Spicy Soy Dipping Sauce, 93
Taro Sauce, 98
teriyaki, 17, 154
Thai Peanut Sauce, 117
tomato, basic, 155
Vanilla Sauce, 129
Sausage
    Portuguese, 51
    Thai Black Rice Risotto, 103-4
Scallions, 32-33
Scallops
    Hawaiian Cioppino, 131-32
    Seafood Full Moon Dumplings,
      68-69
    Seared Scallop Salad with
      Mangoes, 85
    Shrimp and Scallop Spring
      Rolls, 67
Seafood. *See also individual*
    varieties
    Hawaiian Cioppino, 131-32
    Seafood Full Moon Dumplings,
      68-69
    Steamed Opakapaka and Salmon
      with Shrimp Mousse, 120
    varieties of, 36-39
Seared Scallop Salad with
    Mangoes, 85
Seaweeds, 30
Sesame seeds, 54
    oil, 54
    toasted, 153
Shallots, 33
    oil, 153
    sautéed, 153

Shichimi, 28
Shichimi Chicken, 109
Shintaku, Graf, 44
Shiso, 31, 35
Shoyu, 16-17
Shrimp
    Fresh Pasta with Shrimp,
      Pancetta, Anchovy, and Garlic,
      122-23
    Golden Shrimp-Stuffed Tofu, 121
    Hawaiian Cioppino, 131-32
    Kauai, 37
    Seafood Full Moon Dumplings,
      68-69
    Shrimp and Clam Linguine, 126
    Shrimp and Scallop Spring
      Rolls, 67
    Shrimp on a Sugar Cane Stick, 64
    Shrimp Risotto, 128
    Steamed Opakapaka and Salmon
      with Shrimp Mousse, 120
    stock, 154
    Tea-Infused Shrimp Sauté, 127
    Vietnamese-Style Cold Udon with
      Shrimp, 124
Shutome, 38
    Lemon Grass-Crusted Hawaiian
      Shutome, 117
    Ponape Pepper-Crusted Shutome,
      114-15
Sorbet, Mango, 144
Soufflé, Hot Chocolate, 147
Sourness, 2-3, 22-23
Soy sauce, 16-17
    Soy Vinaigrette, 105
    Spicy Soy Dipping Sauce, 93
Spices, 31-35
Spicy Chicken Wings, 66
Spicy Garlic and Black Pepper
    Sauce, 134
Spicy heat, 4, 25-28
Spicy Mango Sauce, 133

Spicy Soy Dipping Sauce, 93
Spring Rolls, Shrimp and Scallop, 67
Sriracha, 26
Steamed Chicken Breast with
    Vegetables, 105
Steamed Opakapaka and Salmon
    with Shrimp Mousse, 120
Stir-Fried Lobster with Spicy Garlic
    and Black Pepper Sauce, 134
Stir-Fried Vegetables, 100
Stocks, 54-55. *See also* Demi-glace
    chicken, 150
    shrimp, 154
    veal, 156
Sugar, 20-21
    cane sticks, 20, 21
    crust, 141
Sushi, Molded, with Unagi and Spicy
    Crab, 71
Sweetness, 2, 18-21
Sweet potatoes, Okinawan
    about, 48
    Okinawan Sweet Potato Mash, 94

T
Tamashiro Market, 37
Tarako, 29
Taro, 49
    Crab and Taro Cakes, 72
    leaves, 156
    rolls, 93
    Taro Sauce, 98
Tarts
    Macadamia Nut Tart, 141
    White Pirie Mango Tart, 146
Tastes. *See* Flavor components
Tea
    green, 34
    Tea-Infused Shrimp Sauté, 127
Teriyaki sauce, 17, 154
Texture, 4-5
Thai Black Rice Risotto, 103-4

Thai Peanut Sauce, 117
Thai-Style Deep-Fried Mullet, 112-13
Tobiko, 29
Tofu
    deep-frying, 46, 79
    draining, 46
    Golden Shrimp-Stuffed Tofu, 121
    MediterAsian Saffron
        Chicken, 111
    pan-frying, 46
    Roasted Duck Salad with Deep-
        Fried Tofu, 7-8, 78-79
    Tofu-Yuba Stir-Fry, 98-99
    varieties of, 46
    Warm Tofu Salad of Wilted
        Greens, 80
Tomatoes, 44
    Cured Salmon and Tomato
        Salad, 83
    peeling, 155
    sauce, basic, 155
    seeding, 155
Tomato juice
    Bloody Mary, 74
    making, 155
Trefoil, 31
Tuscan-Style Pasta, 102

U
Udon
    about, 48
    Vietnamese-Style Cold Udon with
        Shrimp, 124
Uhu
    about, 38
    Chinese-Style Whole Steamed
        Fish, 118
Umami, 3
Unagi, Molded Sushi with Spicy
    Crab and, 71
Uni, 39

V
Vanilla, 129
Veal stock, 156
Vegetables. *See also individual*
        vegetables
    Stir-Fried Vegetables, 100
    varieties of, 40-45
Vietnamese-Style Cold Udon with
    Shrimp, 124
Vinaigrettes. *See* Salad dressings
Vinegars, 22-23
Vinha d'alhos, 93
Visual appeal, 6-7

W
Warabi
    about, 44
    Ahi Salad with Miso Dressing, 82
Warm Tofu Salad of Wilted Greens, 80
Wasabi, 28
Watercress, 44
White Pirie Mango Tart, 146
Wok-Charred Edamame, 62
Won bok, 44
    Ahi Salad with Miso Dressing, 82
    Shrimp and Scallop Spring
        Rolls, 67
Wong, Alan, 86

Y
Yuba
    about, 46
    Tofu-Yuba Stir-Fry, 98-99
Yuzu, 22

Television Show Supporters

Underwriters

THE ISLANDS OF ALOHA

www.gohawaii.com

SUB-ZERO | WOLF

contact the Westye Group-West, Inc. at (808) 485-0909

HAWAI'I FILM OFFICE
Department of Business, Economic
Development, & Tourism

www.hawaiifilmoffice.com

In-Kind Contributors

Aloha AIRLINES

Tommy Bahama

MAC
WORLD'S SHARPEST KNIVES

Hilo Hattie
The Store of Hawaii

All-Clad
METALCRAFTERS LLC

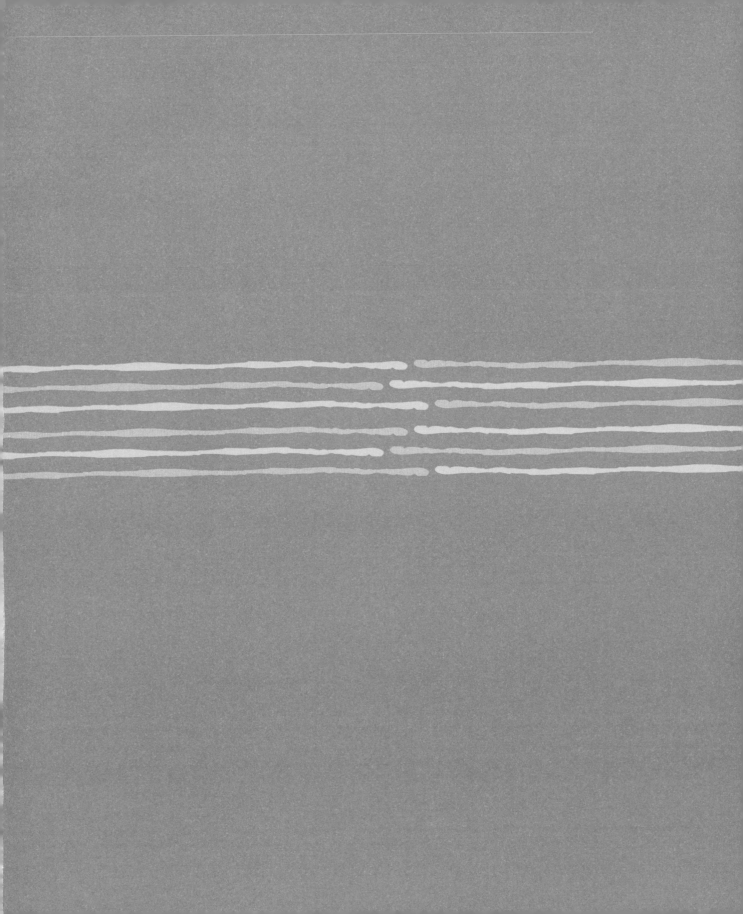

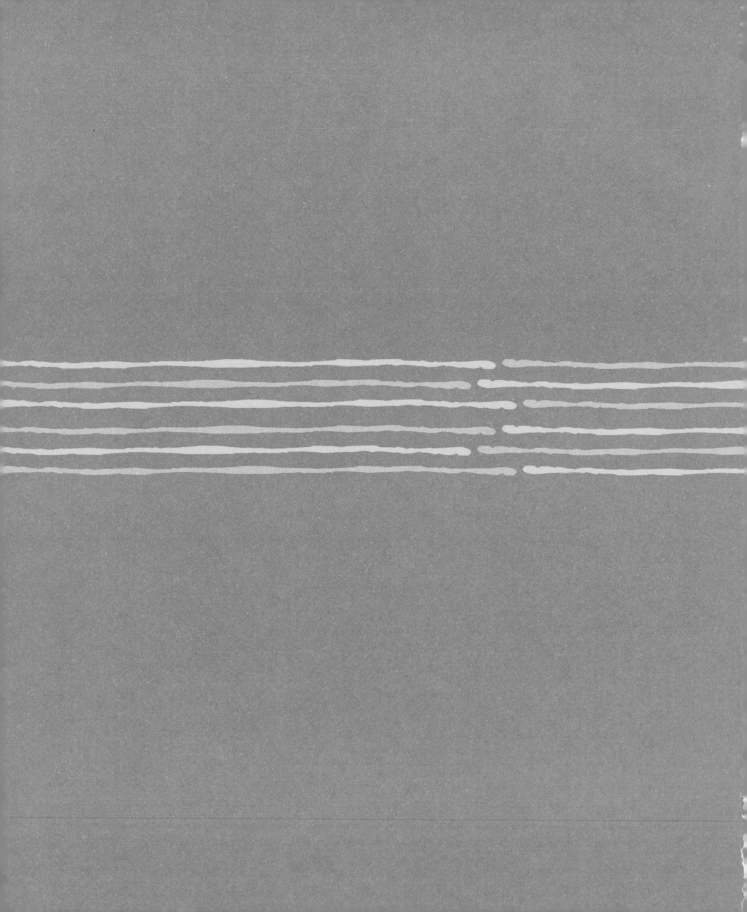